Quotes from celebrities and experts

"Read at the risk of falling in love with Fern and Norman Brooks and their remarkable love story."
—Norman Lear, writer, producer

"...compassionate, caring and deeply moving. I know it will do a lot of good..."
—Peter McWilliams, author

"It's a compassionate and funny view of growing older. It touched me deeply."
—Bea Arthur, actress

"He was the best. She's still the best. Together they were sunshine and laughter. I'm delighted this touching memoir was written—now I can keep a part of them forever."
—Estelle Getty, actress

"It changed my life."
—Barry Flatman, actor

"It was good. Every time I thought it was getting too close, too intimate—the mood would change and I would be moved to laugh..."

—Simon MacCorkindale, actor

"You can pick it up and open it to any page and be engrossed—makes you laugh and makes you cry."

—Barry Lee, TV talk show host

"I loved it. It carried me through and held my interest all the way. Fern is a wonderful writer."

—Ruth Handler, cofounder, Mattel, Inc.

"I cried and laughed but most of all I learned what it truly means to love and be loved."

—Arthur Weingarten, TV writer, author

"I couldn't believe how it made me cry—I'm not like that. It's wonderful."

—Rita Aero, author

"Ruined my makeup and my mascara...I couldn't stop crying...and couldn't put it down. Norman would be so proud."

—Gladys Nederlander, TV producer

"You have no idea of your impact—but I do—because I hear it from my clients and my staff. They tell me whenever anyone is waiting to be picked up or something, they don't want to talk—they just want to pick up a copy of your book and just curl up in a corner and read. You're a real healer—you're helping a lot of people to sleep at night."

—Joann Lautman, director of Our House,
a bereavement center,
Beverly Hills, California

...and from the general public

"I read it in one sitting like an engrossing novel. It is a remarkable love story."

"It was the only book that helped me. The others tried to tell me what to do and how to feel. This one just shared what I was thinking and feeling. It was a great comfort."

"My mother-in-law couldn't thank me enough for the book. She said whenever she feels depressed or lonely, she goes to the book and staris reading and feels better."

"Even before finishing it, I had to pick up the phone and call my wife back home in L.A. and tell her I loved her."

"Just knowing that your kind of relationship is possible gives me hope and a determination not to settle. Thank you for sharing your feelings and thoughts and giving me a little glimpse of what is possible."

"I gave the book to my mother and she said she could have collaborated on it—so many of the feelings expressed were her own. She's starting to read it again and carries it with her."

"It touched my heart, my soul and my memories of my father...a real testimony to the meaning of love."

"Even the appendix is fun to read!"

"Fern Field Brooks is a wonderful writer. I feel like I'm walking the streets of Paris with her when she writes about it."

"I was so moved I read it cover to cover in one sitting. I couldn't put it down and have already recommended it to six friends."

Letters
to My
Husband

By
Fern Field Brooks

CAREER
PRESS
Franklin Lakes, NJ

LETTERS TO MY HUSBAND ISBN 1-56414-185-5, $19.99
Cover design by The Gottry Communications Group, Inc.
Printed in the U.S.A. by Book-mart Press

To order this title by mail, please include price as noted above, $2.50 handling per order, and $1.00 for each book ordered. Send to: Career Press, Inc., 3 Tice Road, P.O. Box 687, Franklin Lakes, NJ 07417.
Or call toll-free 1-800-CAREER-1 (Canada: 201-848-0310) to order using VISA or MasterCard, or for further information on books from Career Press.

Library of Congress Cataloging-in-Publication Data

Brooks, Fern Field.
    Letters to my husband / Fern Field Brooks.
       p.   cm.
    Includes index.
    ISBN 1-56414-185-3 (hard)
    1. Brooks, Fern Field--Correspondence. 2. Brooks, Norman G., 1926-1991--Correspondence. 3. Los Angeles (Calif.)--Biography. 4. Grief--Personal narratives. 5. Bereavement--Personal narratives. 6. Love letters--United States. I. Title.
CT275.B75622L48   1995
155.9'37'092--dc20
[B]   95-18905
                                              CIP

Dedicated to all the loving friends whose support, concern and caring have helped me in this time of grief.

And to Lois de la Haba, without whose promise of help and words of encouragement, this book would never have been written.

And to Michael Spivak, whose enthusiasm and exuberance crystallized my own need and desire to "write a book."

But most of all to Norman G. Brooks, my husband for 11 very special years, and my friend and lover for 23, whose love, support and adulation still shine so brightly that I am constantly enveloped by the feeling and the warmth.

And finally to all those close to me, and those whom I have yet to meet, who have suffered the loss of a loved one—this is for you—because it isn't always easy to share the grief. Sometimes you have to do it in private. This book is for you—to help you reach out and heal the pain.

My husband Norman always used to say—if you have something on your mind, if there are things you want to get off your chest, thoughts you need to express, but are not sure how or when to say them—sit down and write a letter.

He gave this advice to people who were angry, to people who were hurt, to people who were in mourning. "You can talk to the one you love," he would say, "even if that person isn't here."

I didn't know when I heard him say those things—that he was also saying them to me.

Norman, my love,

It's hard to believe this whole thing—this book—started with an overwhelming desire to talk to you—when I sat down in Paris and wrote:

"A letter to my darling husband..."

and then painfully had to add:

"...on the first anniversary of his death."

Part I

*"God grant me the serenity to accept the
things I cannot change—*
the courage to change the things I can—
and the wisdom to know the difference."

Anonymous

Paris, December 19, 1991

Dearest, darling Norman,

I'm sitting here in Paris, in an apartment you would have loved—which has an unobstructed view from almost every room of the golden dome of the Invalides and of the Eiffel Tower when you walk out on the balcony—realizing it's almost a year since you passed away.

I've been going nonstop since that fateful day—partly because it helped not to have to think about things and partly because I had to. I guess now, what with the holidays and all, I'm beginning to take stock.

Paris has been good for me. Somehow being in Europe has taken me back to a previous life—when I lived in Italy, before you—so it hasn't been so painful. There haven't been many memories, except when I'm around the Hotel Lutetia, where we stayed, or on a street we walked together or a store where we shopped.

The city is so beautiful, so stunningly lit, that it is nurturing for the spirit. It's really hard to be depressed with the Eiffel Tower and the Champs Élysées beckoning you to enjoy life. It draws you out in an extraordinary way.

In fact, just weeks after I got here, while I was still living in the hotel, I did something I've never done before in my whole life. It was a Sunday and I got out, went for a long walk, had dinner and went to a movie. All by myself! In my entire life, I've never done that—not even to an industry screening—and I didn't mind at all. I wasn't uncomfortable or self-conscious or anything. I was amazed! I remember years ago wondering how my mother could do things like that all by herself. Maybe it's Europe.

And last night you would have been so proud of me. I heard there was going to be a holiday celebration inaugurating the Winter Olympics and they were closing the Champs Élysées to traffic, and I went! I had come home with packages, and the festivities were being shown on TV, and you know how lazy I can get. But instead of copping out and staying in, I went—gladly, joyously, and partly because I knew you would have wanted to go.

You always enjoyed everything so much—and remembered everything so well—while I kind of sleepwalked my way through experiences, knowing, counting on you to remember them for both of us. This time, I was the one experiencing it for the two of us.

And how you would have loved it! The night air was brisk, but not unbearable. The avenue was lit like high noon for the TV cameras and the confetti covered the street like a white carpet, making it look like it had snowed.

I walked down the middle of the street and looked back at the Arc de Triomphe getting smaller and smaller as I neared the Concorde, and it was magical.

I passed the Hotel Crillon and remembered shooting *Eleanor, First Lady of the World* there and noted it was only 10 short years ago and you had been there, and my mother had been there, and now I was here—alone.

At home (wherever that may be these days), I have dozens of pictures of you smiling out at me in every room. And the love notes you used to leave for me are still all over—in my pockets, in my drawers, in my Day Runner. But last night, in front of the Crillon, I was alone.

And I started to think about that, and the idea of writing/talking to you—which had started brewing in me during the last couple of days—became overwhelming. As did the realization that I am alone. You are not coming back, and that's not the way it was supposed to be. You were supposed to be here with me, for me. We were supposed to grow old together. And now I'm growing old alone and sometimes it seems that it goes faster than when you were here.

As I turned away and crossed the bridge toward home, I thought how much you would have enjoyed walking in the brisk night air. Then I realized that you probably couldn't have—shouldn't have—done it. That the cold night air would have made it difficult for you to breathe. And while I hate not having you here with me, I thank God that he granted you your wish never to be incapacitated or diminished in what you could or could not do. I remember you saying, "When my time comes, I want to go quickly and in my sleep." God gave you that, Normy. And, my God, how gorgeous, how well you looked on the day you died.

Last December, how beautiful you looked in your brand new tuxedo at all those weddings we attended. We buried you in it. Because although we never really talked about death and dying, I remembered you once told me you wanted to be buried in a tux. "I want to go in style, of course," you said. And I remember on December 31, at John and Angela's wedding, as you were going down for pictures as their best man, you kvelled and said to me: "I love this tuxedo—it makes me feel so good."

Several times during the last few months of 1990, you said you wanted only one thing—to be able to celebrate your 65th birthday with me. And, I remember thinking, as you kissed me at midnight on New Year's Eve, "So what's the whole big deal? Here it is January already and March is just around the corner."

Three days later I learned what the whole big deal would be.

Soon, we'll have a brand new baby girl in the family. How you would have loved that. A new little baby to cuddle and hug. I hope and pray this event will help turn these painful holidays into a happy time of year again for your children. They have had too much pain, what with their mother's death three years ago on Christmas Day, and yours last year (actually, this year) on January 3!

They say time heals. I'm not sure what that means. And maybe there will be other loves, other people. But there will never be anybody who loves me, worships and adores me as you did. And I don't think I will ever love anyone as I love you.

Because you know how kooky I am and how I believe in all those mystical things, I thought you'd "visit" me more often. Actually, you've only come to me once in a dream to cheer me up. And you do occasionally talk to me through other people. Like when Jim, our accountant, begins and ends every conversation with the words, "Don't quit!" I know that's you telling me not to walk away from a good job, no matter how much those turkeys get to me. It's you tempering my hot-headedness.

And when I sat down last spring and fired off a memo to one of the executive producers of our series, I know you cringed and said, "Oh, my God, she's writing another one of her memos!" And He turned to you and said, "Don't worry, Normy, she hears you telling her to choose her words carefully and not to back people into a corner without giving them a way out. Living with you, she learned a few things." He was right, of course.

So, I console myself about your lack of "visitations" with the thought that souls who are at peace don't wander around too much.

And so, my darling, rest in peace. Know that you have left the most incredible legacy of life and love. Know that your 10-year-old grandson—who is now 5'1"—remembers you because wherever you went, you talked to strangers and made friends. Know that you are missed by people you never even met, but who have told me how you brightened their day every time you called. Know that you are remembered by people who were receptionists and production assistants—who recall you treated them with the same kindness, respect and interest you accorded their bosses—many of whom are now executives themselves and who are emulating the attitudes and lessons they learned from you.

The letters, my beloved, came in droves. I'm still answering them. You made a difference, Normy. You are a beautiful human being and you are sorely missed by all of us.

I love you.

Your wife,

Los Angeles, January 3, 1992

My beloved husband, my darling Norman,

It's a year today! At first, this morning, when I woke up, I didn't realize that. I got up, got dressed and went about my business. Then in the car a heaviness descended and enveloped me, and wouldn't let me go. And I remembered what day it was.

This evening there was a special memorial service for you, heralded by the full-page ads featuring your smiling face, which I took out in *Variety* and *The Hollywood Reporter*.

Before the services, I took the family, and some of our friends who are family—Marty and Rochelle, Estelle Getty, Michael and Gloria who flew in from New York—to dinner at the Mandarin. God, how you would have loved it, Normy. It was the best Chinese food I've ever had. Everybody raved, and we all kibitzed about how much you loved Chinese food and always kidded that you wished your mom had been Chinese!

This morning I ordered a couple of limos for some of our guests because it was pouring rain. Our services are back on Crescent Heights at Beth El, and you know how difficult parking can be around there. Anyway, Estelle doesn't drive, and that way your daughter Bobbi, who's pregnant now, wouldn't have to, and it turned out to be a really good idea. Because even though by this evening it had virtually stopped raining, the cold, damp night air cut to the bone, just like the pain we were all feeling.

I read my December 19 letter to you at the service—and a lot of people were moved to tears. Some of them came up to me and asked for copies, so Hal Sloane asked if he could reprint it in the temple newsletter. Of course, I said yes. Keeping your memory alive gives me a purpose and makes life bearable. Knowing people are thinking of you, as I am, heals the pain. It means a lot to me. (I didn't know, then, that letter would be the beginning of this book.)

It's funny, you know. In that first letter I complained that you aren't "visiting" me enough, that you aren't "in touch." Since I believe in all of those things, I somehow thought you would always be with me. I thought you would pervade my dreams and walk beside me—a presence I could feel. But you have been strangely silent—except for that time when you "didn't approve." Then you gave me a sign, loud and clear.

There was this man (not unattractive, and the right age) who made it clear he could be interested if I would just let him in. I was toying with the idea, even though he made me feel somehow uncomfortable—and I knew that what I needed now was not someone who would make me feel ill at ease. I needed a man who would comfort me, not pressure me. Someone who would be tender and thoughtful and considerate—like you were all those years. Someone with whom I could let my hair down, who would cuddle me, not someone it was going to be work to be with. (And maybe that's why you interfered!)

Anyway, I decided I should ignore my trepidations and just call to say hello and suggest a cup of coffee. He could take it from there. But as I reached for the phone by the bed, I was startled by a loud noise behind me.

I was alone in the house and couldn't imagine what that noise might have been, so I hesitated before I turned and saw your snapshot—which had been framed and was on our bookshelf for years—lying on the carpet. Puzzled, I looked back at the shelf and realized the photo had to have fallen, making sure it hit the lamp on its way down, in order to cause that almost impossibly loud noise that distracted me from picking up the phone. I gazed at the photo on the floor and realized there had been no breeze, no movement I hadn't made in that room a thousand times before. Nothing. No reason for it to fall at that moment and in that way. So I said to you out loud, "Okay, I get the message. You don't like it, you don't approve, it's wrong, it's too soon. Now, just give me another sign. Do something else! Anything to let me know you're here." But silence echoed in the room and there were no more gestures from the other side. You had made your point and I guess there was nothing else you had to say. Of course, I didn't call or go for coffee on that day.

The service tonight was very moving. People came from all over to let me know they cared. A lot of them I hadn't seen in many years. And people who came were there just for you. People like Richard Marcus, who thought of you as the father figure he would have liked to have. People like Ethel Poirier, for whom you brought flower seeds from France the last time we were there. They came to honor you and mourn you. To let us both know that they missed you and they still cared.

Toward the end of the service, our rabbi Jerry read a poem that brought a lot of tears.

To Those I Love

When I am gone, release me, let me go—
I have so many things to see and do.
You mustn't tie yourself to me with tears
Be happy that we had so many years.
I gave you my love. You can only guess
How much you gave me in happiness.
But now it's time I traveled on alone.
So grieve a while for me if grieve you must
Then let your grief be comforted by trust.
It's only for a while that we must part
So bless the memories within your heart.
I won't be far away, for life goes on—
So if you need me, call and I will come.
Though you can't see or touch me, I'll be near—
And if you listen with your heart, you'll hear
All of my love around you soft and clear
And then when you must come this way alone
I'll greet you with a smile
and "Welcome Home."

Anonymous

Paris, February 26, 1992

My dearest, darling Norman,

Gloria and her daughter Leslie have just left after visiting me here in Paris for a week.

Gloria thinks I should put your photos away. My friend Elisabeth Getter, who was here a couple of weeks ago, thinks the same thing. They say I've created a shrine to you—that it's time to say good-bye.

What they don't realize is that I haven't even begun to come to terms with the fact that you're not here. A lot of times I feel there's been this terrible mistake. That it wasn't meant to be this way...that if you hadn't gone for the angiogram...that if I could just turn back the clock...

You passed away in New York on January 3. By February 4 I was in Toronto prepping the second season of *Counterstrike*. And in that short period of time, there was getting back to L.A., the funeral, sitting shiva, moving out of our office and leaving.

And how I resented going. I remember talking and crying on the phone with your sister Natalie just before I had to leave for the airport and explaining that all I really wanted was to be left alone with my grief. I wanted to hole up and feel sorry for myself, and cry and carry on, but it was as if God, life, whatever (probably you) was pushing me out, saying to me, "You can't! Life goes on, and you must continue with it."

And I remember how overwhelming it was to contemplate a future without you. The enormity would wash over me and I would reject it—push it out of my consciousness. How could I bear it? How could I survive days, weeks, months, without you? So I would turn my attention immediately to some crisis at hand. And, God knows, on *Counterstrike* there were always plenty of them to keep me occupied. So before I knew it, the months had turned into a year.

I went home for the holidays with some apprehension and concern. I thought it would be painful, depressing, too hard to bear. But that turned out not to be the case. The apartment was so full of you. The energy I got from your presence was unreal. It had me bouncing off the walls and somebody finally said to me, "You're living as if he were still here." And I realized I was. I was acting as if you'd just gone out on some mission and would come waltzing through the door any minute.

I was able to give away some of your things. But of course, I only gave away the clothes I didn't like. The things I would have wanted you to get rid of anyway. All your good things are still there. As I sifted through your clothes and made selections, I could hear Michael making fun of me and saying, "Of course you're keeping the good things, because Normy'll need them when he comes back." And I smiled to myself as I rearranged your suits in the closet, and heard your teasing voice ringing in my ears, "Get away from there! Who gave you permission to reorganize my things?" (By the way, would you care to explain that package in your suede jacket pocket, which I thought was a bag of mothballs and turned out to be chocolate-covered maltballs! I thought we were supposed to be on a diet?!)

And then I picked up a pair of your shoes—and dropped them like a hot potato! God, the sense of finality that overcame me when I thought of giving away your shoes! I couldn't do it...wouldn't do it. So I made a mental note to try again next year.

While I was going through your desk at Christmas, I got a phone call from the office. There was some new crisis that cried for my attention and I felt frustrated and angry and put upon, and suddenly, these two round Boynton stick-ons fell out of one of your drawers and made me burst into laughter and tears.

The first one shows a hippo lying on a couch and the caption says, *"I love you more than chocolate itself."* And I smiled because that is so like you and I knew you were sending me a message to ease my pain. But the next one made me laugh out loud.

It's an elephant with turkeys climbing all over him—and the caption says, *"Don't let the turkeys get you down!"* Coming on the heels of that phone call, it was as if you had reached out from wherever you are to comfort me, to help me feel better and get through the crisis. I looked heavenward and thanked you out loud.

I did go out to dinner with someone in New York before coming back here. He was the brother of a terrific woman I met in Toronto last year. And, although he was really very nice, I knew on the phone he would not be for me for a variety of reasons too long to go into—not the least of which was that he was looking to make a life with someone and I was just looking to survive another season of series television. But I remember talking over dinner and hearing that he had already had bypass surgery, and was now having a bout with cancer, and this overwhelming feeling came over me. Oh, no, not again. No more hospitals and doctors and living on the edge...never knowing. I can't do that anymore, not now, not for a stranger.

And more and more I find my thoughts turning to that fateful January night when you passed away, and thinking what might have been.

I've often said that the grief is easier for me because we didn't have a lot of "if only's"—"If only I had told him that I loved him," "If only we had taken that vacation trip," and so on and so forth.

We loved each other, and told each other, and hugged and kissed each other. Wherever we went, we had a fabulous time, and that night we were in the midst of a very good trip. No work, no phone calls, no meetings. You went to bed that night laughing because I was counting on my fingers (as usual) the number of hours we needed to sleep so you could set the alarm. We planned to have a heavy day of shopping. I wanted to compare prices at a cashmere store on Madison Avenue to see if the sweater we bought at Bergdorf's had been a good deal. Little did I know that I wouldn't wear that sweater— because it was purple—for a whole year. It was the first colored thing I put on when I stopped wearing black after the memorial service this January.

But there are other "if only's" and "what if's" that are beginning to haunt me. "If only" we hadn't walked in the cold the night we went to the movies... "If only" we hadn't gone to Jasper last summer where you first felt a twinge. Maybe it was the altitude. Did the frequent flights make a difference? Should we have tried to dissolve the new blockage? Could I have, would I have, should I have done something differently? If only I had...would you still be here? And how come we never talked about a heart transplant?

And how sorry I am that you couldn't get through to your daughter Bobbi that night before you went to sleep. She hadn't been feeling well and you wanted to talk to her. But the line was busy and we finally decided it must have been out of order, so we went to bed.

I remember waking up to the sound of heavy, labored breathing. I thought you were having a nightmare. That in your dream you must be running, running, and I turned to you and kissed you. "Wake up, sweetheart. You're having a nightmare. Wake up, it's okay." But you didn't respond. I reached over you to the lamp on the bedside table between the two queen-sized beds (we always slept in one, very close together), noting the time as I did. It was 1:45 in the morning.

The light went on and I knew. Your eyes were glazed and the movements of your body were mechanical. Mine were too. I called the hotel operator for a doctor. They didn't have one. I dialed 911, trying not to panic. And I was able not to, because you really were not there. It wasn't as if you were awake and gasping for breath, which would have made me hysterical. You were gone and I knew it, but I threw on some slacks and a sweater and went to open the door so the paramedics could get in. I moved like an automaton, somehow knowing what to do, and when your body stopped breathing and you started turning blue, I gave you some mouth-to-mouth resuscitation and your color seemed to come back. I also said: "Don't do this, Normy. Don't leave me, I need you." But I knew it was too late.

And then the paramedics and the cops were there. And I fled the bedroom, unable to bear the thought that they might have to hurt you in some way. And I called Michael and Gloria. And one of the cops came out and told me they had a heartbeat, which surprised me. And they put you on a stretcher and I told them to be gentle with you. The cops—two nice young men—told me they'd drive me to the hospital, and not to worry, and one of them told me about his father and how the paramedics had saved him. And I told Michael and Gloria where we were going. God, how I wish now that I had ridden with you in the ambulance, but they probably wouldn't have let me anyway. I was so afraid they'd have to "open you up," exert pressure on your poor chest that had been invaded too often. When we were on our way to the hospital, we seemed to have lost the ambulance, but the cops said they must have had to stop. And then they reappeared and we drove into emergency and I was being asked questions that all seemed inane and I thought if only I had gone in with you, but I was afraid. And still the cops were comforting and telling me to hang in. The younger one who'd told me about his father said about you, "He's a fighter." Apparently, your heart had stopped in the ambulance and they'd brought you back—as they had in the hotel room—but who knows what state your brain was in by that time.

And then the cops had to leave, wishing me well. Not long after that the doctor came out and explained they had done what they could (I now wonder what that means), and they gave me your personal things. Only they'd forgotten your platinum and diamond ring. And in the middle of everything, I remembered it, and they came back and brought it and it's been on my finger ever since. It was 2:45 in the morning, and "if only" I had gone in. But I was afraid. Afraid to see that they had somehow inflicted pain. Afraid to see you any way but the way I remembered you. Even in death, when I turned on the light—your face was not strained. I couldn't, didn't want to, was afraid to, face what might have been.

And then Michael and Gloria were there, taking me back to the hotel and my attention was taken up by what had to be.

In my more perverse, black-humored moments last year, I would make the joke that the reason you chose to die at this particular time was because you couldn't take another season of my working on *Counterstrike*. That my seven-day weeks, and 18- and 20-hour days were getting to you. I was only half-kidding. I know that you were lonely and that you missed me, that you were jealous of my time away from you. But at least we had those brief hours when I would collapse into bed, snuggle close and feel the warmth of your body giving me strength. I also know how much you enjoyed the things the work was able to bring. On the mantelpiece in the bedroom here in Paris, nestled among various snapshots of you, our family and friends, I have the card you wrote to me from Christchurch saying how much you enjoyed the weekend we shared at Queenstown and the ride on the Shotover Jet! (It's a good thing we hadn't yet heard of "bungee jumping." You probably would have wanted to try that, too!) You would always do that—send cards to me from places where we were together anyway—telling me how much you loved me and how much you cared. And I'd get them days, sometimes weeks, after our trip was over.

Whenever some of the "if only's" get a little too heavy, I read that card from New Zealand, and all the other notes from you that keep me company.

At the very top of the card you wrote:

"FF—we did this!!!"

The picture postcard is of a group of very serious-looking, mostly Asian folks sitting in a Shotover Jet speedboat on a collision course with a cliff. Of course, the photo that someone took of our ride is so much more representative of us. There's you, grinning and waving your arms in the air, enjoying every minute of the experience. And there's me, cringing against the spray and the rain, barely visible from under my parka hood!

The card is dated March 9, 1990 (the anniversary of my mother's death eight years before), and it says:

"*Dearest, darling Fern. This was indeed a special day—and this Christchurch/Queenstown holiday is one I'll remember for a long, long time. So many of my dreams and wishes are coming true, because of you! I just wanted you to know I love you very much. There's no one like you. My heart is yours (fat tush, too!)*" (A reference to our portly state and the reason we were always on a diet!)

You signed it,

"*Always, Norm.*"

My eye always goes to the date when I reread this—and my mind calculates that "the long, long time" ended nine months later.

Los Angeles, March 8, 1992

My love,

We had the unveiling today. It was a small, intimate affair. I didn't schedule it for January when I was home because with Bobbi's pregnancy, we weren't sure how she would be feeling. Also, by postponing till now, I was hoping we could have the baby naming this past Friday— but Bobbi wasn't sure she'd be up to it—and we couldn't leave the decision to the last minute because Jerry had to plan the services. So, I came back now for a couple of days.

But baby Alexandra Noelle, your beautiful new granddaughter, did come to the unveiling today. She's so beautiful, my darling, and how you would have loved her! And Adam, her "big brother," was there. So handsome, so bright and so tall. And your nephew Stan and his wife Tanya and their baby boy were there, too. I bet that surprised you. You always thought he didn't care. But Stan wanted to be there. And then he and Philip hosted the brunch that I had invited everybody to— Natalie, Brian and Cheryl, Michael and Nina, Marty and Rochelle. And I went to the airport to fly to Toronto and Paris right from there! (Talk about cutting things close.)

I wanted to have the unveiling now, before too much time had passed beyond a year. I'll be in Paris till midsummer and that's a gruelling trip, from Paris to L.A. I felt I needed to have this closure without any more delays.

The plaque is nice, Normy. I ran the wording by the family before I ordered it. They all liked it. I think you'd like it, too. It says:

Norman G. Brooks
March 24, 1926 - January 3, 1991
beloved husband, father, grandfather, brother, friend—
he cared, he made a difference, he was the best!

We have a double grave plot. The man at the cemetery was afraid your inscription would be too long—that there wouldn't be enough room for my dedication. I told him not to worry; it didn't matter what they put for me, and who would write it anyway? Natalie said I could just put "Me too." That sounds good to me. What do you think? (Or I can use the description that Tom Backer once used for me, and say: Here lies a "social issues" groupie.)

At the graveside, Jerry read another poem that so echoes how I often feel.

> *Time does not bring relief; you all have lied*
> *Who told me time would ease me of my pain!*
> *I miss him in the weeping of the rain;*
> *I want him at the shrinking of the tide;*
> *The old snows melt from every mountainside,*
> *And last year's leaves are smoke in every lane;*
> *But last year's bitter loving must remain*
> *Heaped on my heart, and my old thoughts abide.*
> *There are a hundred places where I fear*
> *To go, —so with his memory they brim.*
> *And entering with relief some quiet place*
> *Where never fell his foot or shone his face*
> *I say, "There is no memory of him here!"*
> *And so stand stricken, so remembering him.*

Edna St. Vincent Millay

Paris, March 21, 1992

Normy,

Monia Joblin and her daughter Sarah left this morning. It's Saturday so there were errands to run and things to do. Ellen and Joey will be arriving Tuesday morning (your birthday), and your baby brother Philip will be here on Saturday. They will be on their way to Israel to visit their year-old grandson—the Gulf War baby. I still remember the stories Philip told us of how pregnant Pam had to stay in a sealed room with a gas mask on, dying to go to the bathroom, but having to wait until the Scuds finished flying!

Anyway, the baby's adorable and it's a boy, almost the same age as Stan and Tanya's son. So your baby brother is now a grandfather twice over and loving every minute of it! And, at least Stan, Tanya and their baby, Simon, are in California. Israel is so very far away.

∽ ∼ ∽

The apartment always feels very empty when my house guests leave—and I walk the beautiful rooms and look at all your pictures. They are so real, Normy. Your smile is so sweet, and on some I can see your every crinkle, and I reach out and touch the photos and it's as if I can feel the softness of your skin. Your eyes follow me wherever I go—and I don't hold back the tears.

The first year I didn't, couldn't let myself cry much, except occasionally in the car in L.A. And, of course, at the cemetery.

I never before understood the value of cemeteries. But now I know they are places where you can let go, unleash the anguish, feel the pain—without phone calls or doorbells or any other interruptions. Cemeteries make you face the truth. The one you love is gone forever. He may live on in your head, and in your heart, but he'll never be able to hold you, or hug you, again. Even the funeral doesn't bring that reality home the way the cemetery does.

God, Normy, the funeral! It's a bizarre and funny thing—but as they'd say in our Hollywood vernacular, *"You would have loved it!"* You would have been so touched and moved by everyone who came. Norman Lear was there (and he even came to the first night of shiva to be part of the minyan. He's such a mensch.) And Bea Arthur was there, and Estelle Getty and Rod Parker and Lorraine Kenney. (How hard it must have been for her with her husband Pat dying only two short months before in almost the same way!) And so many people I never got a chance to see.

You would think that when you have a funeral as large as ours was—and they knew at Hillside it would be, because we told them they'd have to put extra chairs and speakers outside the Chapel for the overflow crowd— that they would understand people would want to come up to the family and comfort them. Which is exactly what people did as they filed past your coffin.

Anyway, the people from Hillside got nervous because they had scheduled a funeral right on the heels of ours. So after the first few people had come over to pay their respects, they prevented others from coming up to us and hugging us and giving us their condolences! And those places have the audacity to tell people that they care! They are heartless, thoughtless, greedy institutions, people who only care about selling as much as they can to as many people as they can. I was going to write them a letter—and probably still will. In America, even death has become big business!

But, to go on, remember how your beautiful, shy, introverted, insecure daughter Bobbi knocked us out by speaking so eloquently at her mother's funeral? Well, at yours, it was Mark. Handsome Mark, who still looks like he's about 18 years old though he's really "thirtysomething." He was so moving, when he finished the only sound in the chapel was sniffling.

Mark had told me he wanted to get up and say something at the funeral, and of course I said yes. But as you can imagine, since with Mark you never know, I and the rest of the family waited with more than a little trepidation as to just what he would say as he headed up to the bima. None of us was prepared for the dignity and beauty of his tribute to you. My heart went out to him, and how I wish he could have said those things to you in person. How I wish that you could have been there to hear them. It would have been so healing for both of you.

"My name is Mark," he began, "and I wish to speak to you today in memory of my father."

"*My father was a man who truly loved life and the many people he came to know.*

He loved to love, to be in love, and to be loved by others. He loved himself and he really loved me in an epic sort of way.

He loved me so that when we first met, he decided to take me home in his 1958 Cadillac convertible and become my Dad. You see, he adopted me and I imagine it would require someone with a limitless passion for life and an enormous heart to do this. My father's was a heart of gold.

And I grew up more fortunate than most. He provided us with everything. I feel lucky to have known him at all—let alone be his son.

My Dad worked a lot. In fact, he worked all the time, and when he wasn't working on work, he was working on his family, and his family's family. We have a large family and it seemed as though when there was a problem, he was looked up to by all for the answers—and he would have them. My Dad—with his own special philosophy—was always in the center, speaking from experience, always having a solution and speaking the truth.

We once had a laugh on the phone. He was giving me advice on love. I had broken up with my girl in New York. I felt much better and I said, 'Dad, maybe you should go into psychotherapy.'

As a child he made me feel very special, and we were never once made to feel that he viewed me and my sisters as a 'group,' because he maintained a special and separate relationship with each of us, making us feel like individuals.

When I was young, he would take me to Nate 'n' Al's, and then to the barber shop to get our hair cut every Saturday. That was 'our' thing.

And I'll never forget the time he brought me to New York on a business trip. We stayed at the Plaza Hotel. I was 10. And, once when driving home from Texas, we stopped in Las Vegas and saw Evel Knievel jump the fountain at Caesar's Palace and later caught the floor show—Diana Ross and The Supremes.

When I was 13 he put me to work in his factory. (Later that year he gave me a bar mitzvah for 400 people.) It would always amaze me the way he was able to communicate with people. He would make them smile. Even people he didn't know—which would sometimes embarrass me—especially when he would start up a conversation with a young girl, usually about my age, and introduce us. My father was good to me. I know now what he was up to—when I look around this room. My Dad has a lot of friends.

My Dad traveled a lot and when I got older, I began to travel, too. Sometimes we would be in the same city. I loved to see him when he was traveling—New York, Toronto, Paris.

In Paris once, we were talking about how special my nephew Adam, his grandson, is and he said: 'Children. Whatever you do, don't miss out on that.'

My Dad was very generous and he knew me. Whenever I needed a $100—I knew that all I had to do was ask him if I could borrow a $20.

I always wanted to make my Dad really proud of me and have been trying to become a millionaire since the age of 16. I wanted to put him on easy street.

Well, a couple of days ago, my Dad died—somewhat prematurely. I still have far to go and much to say to him. I hope he knows what he's doing—'cause I don't know if I'm ready to be without my Dad—even though he will always be with me. I know my Mom is, and you two can hear me. I just wanted to say I love you."

And then your son stepped down, my beloved husband, and I so wished I knew how I could help this beautiful young man who is your son—who needs so much, and seems to be going about everything in the wrong way. How can I make him understand that he doesn't need to be a millionaire to earn the love and respect he so yearns for? How can I teach him to reach out—not to ask—but to give love and care to another human being? So many things seem to stand in his way. And now he must live with the idea that he never lived up to what he thinks your expectations might have been. How can one make him understand how much you loved him? How can one help heal that much pain?

Then our rabbi, Jerry, who loved you so much, called on me.

A number of people were surprised that I could, or would want to, get up and speak. But as Mark had pointed out, the room was filled with friends. I wanted them to know how it had been.

I looked at the crowd that spilled out into the courtyard (chairs and external speakers had been set up for the overflow we expected) and started to speak.

"I had thought I would be able to do this extemporaneously. But then I got nervous—so I jotted down some of the things I wanted to say to you today.

Many of you have expressed the desire to say something. And if Norman had his choice—he would want to hear from each and every one of you. But at these funeral parlors, they run these things on a schedule that's tighter than a television show's, and we have a very limited time to do all of this. That's why I hope you'll come by today, or during the week, to share your thoughts and your memories with me, and to help celebrate Norman's life. Each of us shared special moments and experiences with him and the sum of those experiences is what Norman was all about.

Norman loved life, he loved people, he loved being loved by everyone. And he loved me, unconditionally, and without reservations. I know how special, and how rare, that is.

We had arranged our lives so that we could spend almost every minute of every day together. Many relationships would bristle under that kind of proximity. Ours flourished. We were best when we were glued at the hip—walking down Fifth Avenue, the Champs Élysées, or the harbour road in Wellington, New Zealand.

He was my ballast, my strength, my wisdom. He was my husband, my lover, my best friend—and I know he will continue to guide me, to be with me, until we're together again.

He was special. But you all know that because you all loved him and he loved you. I don't need to eulogize Norman, or review his life for you. I want to tell you something else.

Norman was an optimist. To him the glass was always half-full—versus my vision of half-empty. But this past year even I had to admit we had a good one. There's some irony in *that. Like the Russian proverb that says: 'God forbid it should get any better,' implying that somehow things will get jinxed.*

But there's comfort in it, too—and I want to share that comfort with all of you because it does ease the pain.

I want you all to know that Norman went out on a real high. He looked great, he felt great. We were having a fabulous vacation, spending every minute of every day together, just the way we like it. And he went the way he wanted to go—quickly and peacefully, in his sleep.

He was very happy. We were very happy. We'd had a wonderful year seeing new parts of the world together—and were beginning to see the light at the end of the tunnel after a couple of pretty tough years. I guess God decided it was the right time for Norman to keep walking into that light. So, while I shall miss him dearly, I thank God that He gave Norman almost 65 years of quality life, and that he did not have to suffer. Or deteriorate into an invalid, or become a burden in any way—which would have been intolerable for Norman.

In early December he had the opportunity of spending a weekend alone with Adam, our grandson. His sister Natalie spent some special time with him in New York this fall. Robin, his oldest daughter, and her friend Joan came down for the Hannukah-Christmas holidays, stayed with us, and we shared two very special evenings with the rest of the family—his daughter Bobbi Lee, his son Mark, our son-in-law Al Verdi and his family.

On New Year's Eve, Norman was best man at the wedding of our friends, John McPherson and Angela Mancuso—and it was a magical evening.

The day he died, we went to a matinee with our friend Gloria, and then were joined at dinner by her husband Michael and our friend Larry Keith.

To the very last minute, Norman basked in the glow of our love for each other, our families and our friends. He was happy—and I hope knowing that will bring all of you the comfort it is bringing me."

~ ~ ~

Almost everybody came back to the house after the service. We put the large photo of you (which Sandy Pollock had had blown up and which had stood on an easel by your closed coffin for the funeral), up on the mantelpiece in the living room.

In fact, the photo is still there, except for the few months that Lynne Thomson rented the apartment last year. She took it down while she was there. I mentioned it to Michael and Gloria, and Michael kidded me that I would probably have given her a rent reduction if she had agreed to leave it on the mantelpiece. I laughed, but that's actually the case!

So lots of people came by to share after the services, and I loved them for it. Because every story, every reminiscence helped to keep your memory alive. Your presence filled our hearts and buoyed us. Marty Litke told me how special my words at the service had been. He said, "Here you are giving us comfort when we should be giving it to you."

~ ~ ~

I thought going to Toronto in February would be easy. But it was really tough. Except for a couple of times right after your angiogram when you stayed home, we had always traveled together. In the last dozen years, since your bypass and our decision to work together, we had been the "Bobbsey twins." Now, suddenly, I was alone and even though I was going to a new hotel, on a new assignment, your absence was excruciating.

In fact, that's the way it's been all through this year. The things I think are going to be so difficult turn out to be a breeze and the things I think are going to be easy wind up tearing me apart with pain.

That's all for now, Normy. I've just realized that your brother Philip will be here next week—and I've just taken a look at my slippers you wanted me to get rid of while you were still alive. (If you thought they were ratty then—you should see them now!) So, in honor of the first male family member to come and stay in my Paris apartment—and actually more for you than for him—because I know how much these dirty, ratty slippers would embarrass you—I'm off to replace them. My first shopping spree in gay Paree!

I love you—always have—always will.

Jerri

Paris, March 24, 1992

My darling,

It's your birthday—the second one since you're not here.

Ellen and Joey arrive in Paris later this morning. Last year, Michael and Gloria flew up to Toronto to be with me. It was something they decided they wanted to do when they were at the funeral in January. They've shared so many of your birthdays with us during these past years, and now we would be celebrating it without you. Although your loss and the pain were still very fresh for all of us, none of us had truly accepted that this was all for real.

In fact, when the production company offered me a ticket to a jazz concert for Saturday night, my secretary, Keitha, asked if I wanted her to see if she could get a couple of extra tickets for Michael and Gloria. I automatically corrected her by saying, "But, we'll need *three* more." It wasn't until I noticed she was looking at me sort of funny that I realized what I had said.

And, on Friday night, when the waiter at Il Posto, our favorite Italian restaurant, brought only three glasses of water, I almost blurted out that we needed four. And, of course, Michael got really upset when he learned that we had only reserved dinner for three.

Yes, Michael, Gloria and I were quite a threesome that weekend. You would have really laughed at us. We did everything as if you were still there. We picked restaurants that served your favorite foods—Italian at night, dim sum during the day! I don't think we said one sentence that didn't have your name in it. It was Normy this and Normy that.

But Saturday night, your birthday dinner, really took the cake. I thought you'd like La Scala. Remember? The pretty restaurant we wandered into early one weekend night and said we should come back to? We did—to celebrate your 65th! We got all dressed up the way you would have liked, and Gloria looked stunning as usual. Actually, Michael and I didn't look so bad either. And as we left my hotel suite, Michael, still a little peeved that we wouldn't have four places set for dinner, insisted I bring a picture of you. So, I took the snapshot of you as an elegant congressman in our CBS film *The Littlest Victims*, and off we went.

The restaurant, as you know, is very quiet, elegant and sedate. We had a lovely, prominent table in the center of the room, and were in good spirits as we ordered a round of drinks. Your presence among us was palpable, and though none of us said it, we all had this feeling that you would be joining us any minute. Then, as the waiter brought our drinks, I took out your photo and put it where your place would have been.

We never anticipated the effect this was going to have.

Within seconds tears were streaming down Gloria's cheeks, and mine weren't far behind. Michael started to sob out loud and God knows what the people in the restaurant were beginning to think! The thought of this turned my tears to giggles—and I quickly seized the photo and slipped it into my bag before La Scala had three very hysterical people on their hands.

You see, with your picture on the table, we couldn't pretend that you'd be walking in. It brought all the painful reality to us in a wave. And, as Gloria put it the next day, instead of dealing with it and talking about your death, we simply put your picture away.

Sunday evening after they left, I sat down to write thank-you notes to people who had written and made contributions in your memory. (I am still doing that to this day!) I stumbled onto a PBS rebroadcast of the Pavarotti, Carrera, Domingo concert at Rome's Terme di Caracalla. The music washed over me (as did thoughts of how you would have loved this show) along with a lot of tears. For another brief span of time—moments really— there was no denying what I knew to be.

Sometimes, at various points in those early months after your death, I would wonder why I needed to be here. What purpose or meaning did my life have? Why should I go on with this mundane, day-to-day existence? Especially, why should I go on with it without you?

I don't mean this to be melodramatic, or to say that I had to live only through you. I've made my mark in this world—in this life—so it wasn't like the crisis I had in my 30s—before I met you, when after my first divorce and a dead-end love affair I was convinced that without children and without a career, I was worthless.

Ironically, now, it was almost the opposite. There seems nothing left to do. I've had the career, I've earned the awards. In our own small way in our work with the disabled, we've affected change, made a difference, left a legacy.

Now I wasn't doing any of those things—and although I had tried to inject a little social conscience into *Counterstrike*, was supervising a television series all there was going to be? If I didn't have you to share the benefits with, what meaning was there going to be?

I thought about the poem I wrote for you when you were struggling desperately with all the changes in your life. I was trying to tell you, to help you understand, like I hope Mark will someday be able to understand, that it's not that difficult to find the things that will bring us peace, that will make us happy. Remember it?

> *I want to watch sunsets,*
> *count stars in the sky,*
> *Get drunk with that feeling*
> *like a Rocky Mountain high.*
> *I've been the world over,*
> *my love—so have you,*
> *Now help me watch sunsets*
> *and taste morning dew.*
> *The magic is in us,*
> *our world is right here,*
> *Come help me watch sunsets*
> *with the wind in our hair.*
> *Let's walk on the shoreline*
> *and write in the sand.*
> *Come help me watch sunsets.*
> *Come—hold out your hand.*

I recall the images that brought those thoughts to me, the things I wanted to do with you. The fact that I didn't think we needed a lot of money to do them. The day in Mexico when you were giggling and writing "I love you" in the sand. I thought to myself as I watched you: "This is the harassed president of a national menswear company with three factories and more than 600 employees?"

But we didn't get to watch enough sunsets, my darling, and now I'm afraid of all the ones I'll be seeing without you.

It happens every time I see a travel brochure of a beautiful place and think I have to see that, I must go there. And then the thought of going there and being there without you makes my heart ache. It breaks with pain and I want to cry out and lash out because it's not fair. How can I stand the beauty without you? How can I bear the pain?

It wasn't too many months after thinking those thoughts that I started smoking again. Not seriously. I never was a serious smoker, but I was having a particularly difficult day. We were still in Toronto and I thought to myself, "What difference does it make, anyway?" So I started just smoking other people's cigarettes. And not as much as when I gave it up almost 10 years ago (just before my mother died and I saw what they had to do in the hospital to drain the phlegm from her lungs and decided it wasn't worth it) just when things got really tense.

And, of course, a lot of people on our show in Canada smoke—not to mention everyone in France—although it does seem to be a little less than the last time we were here. (Jean-Pierre's even given it up. Again!) And I've come to realize it's not just to relieve the tension, or not to eat.

Part of it is oral gratification. I miss the kissing, Normy. You were such a great kisser. I long to have your lips on mine, and drown in the warmth of your embrace. I know why they used to call it "soul kissing"—because when our lips and tongues combined, it was as if you were reaching into the very depths of my soul. My toes tingled, my knees gave way and my body melted into yours. We were as one.

I miss you Norman—more than I can say.

Fern

Normy,

Philip, Ellen and Joanna just left for Israel and the house is empty again.

I've told myself and all our family and friends that I am eager to share this lovely apartment and Paris with them because it is, after all, probably a once-in-a-life-time opportunity. But sometimes I wonder if I'm not also trying to keep the house—and the days and nights—filled, so I don't have to think about the fact that I'm filling them without you.

Last year I was able to do that with my work. But I went through a lot of shit on the job at the beginning of this year—so I can't bury my head in "that sand" anymore. Things have settled down there now, and they're better, and I'm calmer. But I can no longer use *Counterstrike* to dull the pain. It's "only a television show" in the paraphrased words of the great Hitchcock, and it's not even "my" series, so I'll do the best I can. But I have to take stock of my life, and figure out where the road leads from here.

I'm no longer questioning why I have to be here without you the way I did in the beginning. I somehow know that there is a reason why you were taken—or decided to go—when you did, and that I still have something to do, someone to help. That my work here isn't finished.

Funny, the way life works. There's no question in my mind that there is a plan, a purpose—that things happen for a reason. After all, look how close we came to not meeting the night we did. And look at all the things that came from that—an Academy Award nomination, the way our industry perceives disabled performers, a Distinguished Service Award from the President of the United States, an Emmy and countless other awards, shaking hands with the Pope, meeting Rosalyn and Jimmy Carter at the Health Symposium we attended, working with a lot of stars and famous people. Who would have ever dreamed of things like that?

And you found the warmth, affection and love you so longed for, while I found a man who didn't feel threatened by me and who didn't put me on the defensive, who gave me the courage and the encouragement, sometimes in spite of myself, that helped me to achieve.

All this, from a young woman who had been trapped in two failed relationships, who felt so worthless during that period in her life that she couldn't even read *The New York Times* classifieds silently, much less go for a job interview, and who would often walk the streets of New York City, begging to be committed just to get rid of the pain. God, I was a mess when you met me!

And you, restructuring a company, "factored" up to your eyeballs, drowning on the work treadmill, and not quite 40!

Elia Kazan had already written the scenario you were living. Remember, I gave you a copy of *The Arrangement* shortly after we met? About the guy who's going through a midlife crisis, falls in love, and basically winds up with a life not much different from the one he leaves. Only, if I remember the story correctly, love was what made the difference. (Those were the days before I started working in television and stopped reading!)

It wasn't an accident that we two should meet. As I often said to you (and how you loved to hear it), you were the man for whom I had "waited all my life." You, my darling, were the man for me. We were made for each other. My mother used to say—quoting from the old Russian proverb, "God sits upstairs and pairs off people downstairs." And your mom used to say, "For every pot there's a cover," if I remember you quoting her correctly. Whatever the saying, we were made for each other—we both loved loving so much. How can I contemplate a life without you?

It has occurred to me that this is the first time in my life that I am truly "free." There has always been someone there for me. Even if it was an unhappy love affair, there was always someone that I wanted, or who wanted me.

When you lose a spouse, and you're not pushing 100, people are forever telling you how you have a whole life in front of you, how you'll find someone new, how they did and look how well it worked out.

What they don't tell you, or perhaps don't realize, is that they lost their spouses years ago and the "new" partner they're talking about has been with them 20 or 25 years. Or he's a guy who's married someone 20 years younger than he is and no one thinks that's strange. But for a woman in her 50s—well, things change. (Hell, look around. It's hard for a woman at any age!)

I was telling Ellen this the other day: I remember the feeling that came over me one day, way before your death, when I realized I was suddenly too old for something. That there was something actually, and unexpectedly, beyond my reach!

It came as a shock to someone who was always the "baby in the crowd"—and who always got what she really wanted. It was about childbearing.

Always being the youngest among your friends means to be truly stunned the day you meet someone who's younger than you are—who was born after you. But for someone who always thought she could do anything, anytime "if I just really want to," it came as an even bigger shock when I had to say to myself, "No, you can't."

The realization came to me one day in L.A. We were driving somewhere and I saw some young children at play. My thoughts turned to how many friends we had who were just starting families—older men who were starting second ones, younger couples who were on their first. And, out of the recesses of my mind came the thought, "Well, if I really want to, we can do that, too." And suddenly the realization came: "No, you can't—not anymore! You're too old for that!"

I felt as if someone had punched me in the stomach! Oh God! That's true, I thought. I can't. That time has passed. There is actually something that I can no longer do. It's gone forever, beyond my reach and that means there are other things now that I can no longer do. I had no idea that day as I sat next to you in the car and gazed at your gorgeous profile how many things would soon be "beyond my reach."

I guess I never realized the biological clock was ticking because I was too involved in my love affair with you to worry about it. (Besides, when we're young, we always think that we're invincible, immortal, that we'll go on forever.)

Regrets? No, I don't think so. I think our life together was the way it was meant to be. It's just that it's funny to find myself at this juncture in my life—alone, at a time when I must learn to deal with the things I can no longer do. A situation I probably wouldn't have to deal with if you were still by my side.

Now I can understand how frustrated my mother must have been that I didn't sympathize with her preoccupation about growing older. I considered it empty vanity. She would warn me that I would get old, too. "Only you don't get old in your head," she would say.

Boy, is that ever true! In our heads—as you and I often said to each other—we feel ageless. You often marveled that you didn't feel as if you were over 60, and how many times you told me I looked just like a little girl. And to this day, I don't feel like I'm over 50!

Remember my 50th birthday on Rob and Mona's magnificent yacht? I was so excited and getting such a kick out of being half a century old! It was like when I was in my 40s and needed my first pair of reading glasses. I was so thrilled because I felt I was finally "grown up." Well, now I don't think it's quite so kicky to be over half a century old, and it really pisses me off that I can't see a bloody thing without my reading glasses! It makes me feel so damn dependent!

I guess Elizabeth Taylor and women like Sophie Tucker and Marlene Dietrich can/could get any guy they wanted whenever they wanted—no matter what their age. But it comes as a tremendous shock when men around you are suddenly flirting with someone else, especially when you were always the one they went after.

And then you have to ask yourself, "Yes, but when was that?" And the answer is, "A lot of years ago." It's funny, but what happened was I lost interest in other men when I found you—and a lot of years went by. Like the song says in *Fiddler on the Roof* when the kids are getting married: "I don't remember growing older—when did they?"

There are some women, like my Aunt Yara, who truly fit the grand tradition of women with a capital "W," who never stop looking at men, flirting and caring about makeup and clothes and how they look. And I started out like that and my mother was so worried that I would take after Yara, because I looked like her. My mother considered her a "run-around" who got the first divorce in the family in that generation, and had affairs. We're talking about the '30s here, before the sexual revolution, not after! (And you wondered why my mother and my aunt were always at each other's throats and hated each other so passionately!)

I guess there are some similarities between Yara and me, because I was the first divorce in the family in my generation, and the first to "live in sin" with someone. And I was certainly an incorrigible flirt in my teens, but somewhere along the line I started to change. And every man in my life brought about another change.

I surely was a budding "JAP" (Jewish American Princess) when I arrived in Rome at the age of 21, with Stan, my husband of three years. It was Aldo, the man I later fell in love with, who set me thinking about other values. One day he saw me reading *Babbitt* and asked me what it was about. I thought for a couple of seconds, couldn't tell him, and finally answered, "Nothing." He laughed, shook his head, and said, "Fern, books are never about 'nothing.' They are always about something. You have to think about what the author is trying to say."

I saw what he meant right away. More than any of my teachers, he made an impact. The process of change had begun.

Not that I was totally "empty" before that. By the time I was 15, I had read every book on the psychology shelves in the library (which made me realize early on that when my parents told me they were "doing it all for me," that was a crock. It threw me for a loop for a minute—and didn't always stand me in good stead in later years—but from that moment on, I always knew somewhere in the back of my head that we never really do things for other people. We do them for ourselves, because they fit into our scheme of things).

So even though all through my teenage years my mother and I were avid readers and had philosophical discussions deep into the night when my father was away on one of his many trips—or after he died— looking pretty, dressing up, having a nice home and keeping up with the Joneses were still uppermost in my mind then.

Thus, when I left my first husband Stan, a couple of years after that fateful conversation with Aldo about

Babbitt, I still only took pots, pans and linens. (Although I did use the meager financial settlement I got from Stan to go back to school.) But by the time I left my second husband Konny, I had evolved to the point where I took books, a typewriter, my sportscar and, of course, my guitar and the two cats! (It was, after all, the late '60s, and Holly Golightly was my ideal.) Anyway, clearly possessions, material things, were beginning to take a backseat to my spiritual and creative evolution.

And somewhere along the line between marriages and affairs, I lost interest in a lot of makeup, jewels, clothes and flirting with the opposite sex. Because none of the men who crossed my path were ever as interesting as the ones with whom I was already involved.

And I was involved with some man, in some way, for most of my life—until now.

When I was 14 there was Julie—who went from being my "big brother" to becoming the "man of my dreams." How different my life would have been if I had married him. But he went off to college and I went off to sing.

So, on the rebound, I married Stan just after turning 19. The good-looking, self-centered, intelligent attorney with the interesting career, who didn't mind transferring to Europe so I could continue to try and sing.

Thus I met Aldo—the most disruptive and formative affair of my life—when I was just 21. And Konny came along when I was 27. You entered my life when I was 33.

Although there were a couple of months between my breaking up with Julie and meeting Stan, the other relationships criss-crossed and overlapped—without a moment in between. So this is really the first time since my teens that there hasn't been an important male presence in my life. And now, here I am, without a man I'm interested in, suddenly "too old" for a number of things.

It's all really strange—a bizarre series of events, and circumstances, that having you beside me would make a lot easier to live through. You see, the face is wrinkling. I remember spotting the first one—just forming—as I looked into my compact mirror on a flight some years ago and thinking, "Whaddaya know about that?!" (I thought it was funny!) My mother was right—I'm not immune—I'm gonna get old, too. But at the time you were sitting right next to me, and every time you turned to look at me, or leaned over to kiss my hair, you made me feel so beautiful, I could afford to be cavalier about it. I could treat it like I had done with reading glasses. Then, it was fun to find a wrinkle because it meant the process of life was continuing and you and I were going down the road together.

Now I'm walking it alone, and getting old is not as much fun as I always thought it would be. The road looks lonely, and I'm afraid.

I think flying all over the world, which I'm doing more than ever now, accelerates the aging process—all that dry air on the planes. (They ought to give worker's comp for that, don't you think?) The wrinkles seem to be coming fast and with a vengeance. And the body is actually sagging in some places and it's hard to muster the energy to try and do something about it, or rationalize the need. I remember on that last trip to New York, one night you cupped my face in your hands and said, "Altachka, you're getting a wrinkle." And I said, "Lots." And you said, "We're getting old." And I said, "Oh no! Not you!" Because in my eyes you were more gorgeous than ever. But, my darling, if you were beginning to see my wrinkles—how prominent they must look to strangers.

And how ironic that the first time in my life I am truly free, without a man or love interest to inhibit me, it's a time of AIDS, and an era when a torrid one-nighter or love affair with a dashing stranger could be a matter of life and death.

We used to talk about what a terrible time it is to be young and single. It's an even worse time to be widowed and growing old. What happened to the promise of "the best is yet to be"?

When I first came to Paris last fall, I made it a point to go visit some of my old friends. I especially wanted to see my friend Arrigo in Florence because I found out he was very ill.

We were both so excited to see each other after all these years. So there I was waiting for him in the first-class lounge at the railway station—and we almost missed each other. Because he came in looking for a 16-year-old girl and I saw a frail, shuffling old man!

I went to see Aldo, too. He's married now and we had the best day. Jerry (another mutual friend from those wonderful years so long ago that I feel like they happened yesterday) came and Branka was there and the years fell away and we all gave each other a priceless gift—memories of our youth. You see, in our eyes we were the people we were when we met. Only old friends can do that for each other. For our new friends only know us as we are, but old friends remember us the way we used to be—a way we'll never be again.

It's funny how life, time, years change the perspective of things. Driving back from Aldo's that day, Jerry told me how crazy Aldo had been about me—how he used to talk to Jerry about me! I always thought it was basically a case of unrequited love on my part. He didn't care enough about me. I mean, that's why I left Italy— because that love, that relationship, wasn't going anywhere. (Or was it because in the larger scheme of things, I had to leave in order to eventually meet you?)

So Aldo was really crazy about me? And he used to agonize to Jerry about how I could be staying with Stan? I would've jumped off the Empire State Building for Aldo. Why didn't he tell me how he felt all those years ago, instead of telling Jerry?

I had some other revelations and closed some other chapters in my life as well this year.

Remember the time we stopped in Boston on our way to Paris? I told you I had an old boyfriend living there. Since we had a three-hour layover and you were reading and I was bored, I said I was going to see if he was listed and call him. And you, of course, said, "Go ahead." So I did. The first number under the last name (there were only two listings) was a young woman's answering machine (his daughter, I found out) and on the second number a man answered and when he acknowledged who he was, I said, "Well, this is a voice out of your past." He said, "And I know exactly who it is!" I was floored! It had to be 35 years since we had spoken and I wouldn't have recognized his voice in a million years!

We had a nice chat. He told me about his kids and his wife, and that he traveled and occasionally came out West. I invited him to call us and it was all very pleasant—but I was really shook up when I came back to you in the waiting room. I mean, to have someone recognize your voice—and tell you he's never forgotten you after all those years—is a very unnerving experience, especially since I had married on the rebound the first time around because of my unrequited love for him! Julie had been the first major love of my life—and everyone I've ever loved has been cast in his image.

You listened to my story about the phone call, smiled and told me you, too, would have recognized my voice after many years. You were so in love with me it never surprised you that others loved me. I frowned at you, a little ill at ease, as you turned back to your paper and I immersed myself in memories of those very distant years.

Julie was a teddy bear—and every man I've ever really loved has been like him. Strong but cuddly—someone who could smother me in his arms. I remembered he used to call me "Kitten" and started out being the older brother I always wanted, but never had. I was 14 and he was 16 when we met. I was crazy about him—he was brilliant, good-looking, Jewish and well-off. But he treated me like a little girl, so I became his best friend. He used to confide in me about all his girlfriends, and I'd be his spokesperson to them, if necessary. Then sometime after my father died (when I was 17), the relationship changed from "brother" to the man of my life. And for a while, it was great. But he was too mixed up and I was too young and my mother decided to take me to Europe under the pretext of furthering my operatic singing studies. In retrospect, I think she probably just wasn't ready to lose her "little girl." And Julie was going off to college—the beginning of the end.

Anyway, last summer, Philip, Ellen and Joanna were going to be in Boston for a medical convention. It was over a weekend, and on Philip's birthday, so I said I'd meet them, since I'd be back in Toronto by then, and we could celebrate it together.

I also called Julie and reached his wife. She explained they couldn't join us for brunch or dinner because they were going away on the weekend to visit their grandchild. But she gave me another number where I could reach him. Turned out they were separated (not the first time) and we got to talking and he started saying things like how he'd never forgotten me and had never stopped loving me, and had often wondered what might have been. I said, "Hold it! We're remembering this differently. I got married on the rebound from you," I reminded him. And he mentioned a letter I had written to him when I separated from my first husband. I replied, "Yeah, and you never answered it!" And he told me he had come looking for me some months after receiving it—only I had left New York by then!

And, my God, he sounded so unhappy, so depressed, my heart went out to him and I felt drained.

The feeling stayed with me, so some days later I called back, and we had a very long talk. He said (just like you did when we first met and you told me the whole story of your life) that he couldn't understand why he was opening up like that, and talking about all sorts of intimate things. I reminded him that we were old friends. No matter what, that would never go away.

Of course, you would have been on the next plane to Toronto, but he's either too afraid or too self-involved. Anyway, we didn't see each other until this spring— when I was meeting Monia and Sarah in Boston to join their flight to Paris. I went a day earlier (that was my vacation between seasons two and three) and Julie and I had dinner. It was a nice evening. Comfortable. Not like 40 years had gone by since we last saw each other. But the thing that surprised and troubled me most of all was that I couldn't find the boy in the man. He said he would have recognized me anywhere. And I wouldn't have recognized him at all. Even as I sat and gazed at him, I just couldn't see the young man that I had known so many years ago. I wonder if it's because of all his sadness and his pain?

Before I went to Boston, when I was in L.A., I pulled out his letters and memorabilia from all those years ago. (You remember, I'm the one who never throws anything away.) It was interesting because those souvenirs are a portrait of a relationship—how it grew, changed and self-destructed. The letters go from, "I'm so proud to be telling the guys in the dorm about my 'little sister' (referring to my singing career), signed, "Your big brother"; to the one about my father's death and how badly he felt because a month had gone by before he had written; to the ones about how good and how special I made him feel; to a more and more alienated relationship, with a note finally asking me to return his ring!

It's fascinating to look at and contemplate all these things with the knowledge, wisdom and hindsight of so many years.

Versailles, May 1, 1992

Normy,

I'm at the Trianon Palace in Versailles and there's going to be a sunset soon.

The view from my room is extraordinarily pastoral—like a painting by a Dutch master (not unlike some of the vistas we had from rooms on our trip through Scotland)—and the bleating of the sheep drifts into the room through the open window.

Earlier I leaned out of the mansard window and surveyed the luscious green meadow, the rolling hills and the bushy green trees and I could feel you come up behind me and look over my shoulder, as you would have done if you were here.

You'd like this place. It's a brand-new spa and today I had a thermal Jacuzzi, a seaweed wrap and a massage. It's a holiday weekend in France, so I'm trying to use it to brainwash myself into some kind of healthy living.

The direct smoking I've been doing, as well as the passive smoking (although I've noted a marked decrease in smoking in public places here in France, it hasn't reached our industry yet) has really begun to affect me. I can feel the rawness in my throat and the phlegm building up, and yesterday I told myself there are easier, faster ways to commit suicide. And I looked at your photo—and reached out and touched it and wondered about being together again.

At home, Los Angeles is in flames. So is San Francisco and Atlanta, and I think the violence is spreading to Chicago and other cities, too.

It's a reaction to the Rodney King verdict—the black man who was beaten by the L.A. police and somebody got it on videotape. I don't remember if you were still alive when it happened.

Our country, and the world, are a mess. It makes you want to turn your back on all of it. But then something emerges, people respond, and hope springs eternal...until it starts all over again.

Paris, May 14, 1992

My dearest, beloved husband,

Yesterday was our anniversary. It would have been 13 years! Having finally found each other, we shouldn't have had to part so soon. Too soon.

It was a strange day for me. At first I didn't realize what day it was. Then it came to me and I understood why I felt so despondent, depressed, at odds. By the end of the day I had the most violent sore throat. It's still slightly sore today, but it's mostly gone away.

I told you the last time I wrote that I'm no longer questioning why I have to be here. That I understand I still have more work to do. I still have to make a difference. But I'm not sure how, and I'm still torturing myself—as I tortured you—about where I should be living. Or rather, where, and how, I'd like to live out my life.

A couple of months ago—this winter—en route home from the location one night, one of the actresses asked me where I lived. I hesitated—honestly not knowing what to answer her. After all, since we went to New Zealand to do the Ray Bradbury show in January of '90—I don't think I've been home a total of eight weeks in the last two years. Simon MacCorkindale, who was in the car with us, felt my dilemma and filled in the gap for me. "She lives in her head," he said. And I laughed—and marvelled at how well he knew me—because that is so true! That is exactly where I live.

Our world is a mess, my darling, as I mentioned before. South Central L.A., and all around it, has been burned, like in the 1960s riots, only worse. A curfew was imposed and people were afraid to leave their houses. Our politicians are all caricatures, and our government is a shambles. There is the kind of discontent that spawned the Hitlers of the past, and the kind of economic depression that nurtured them. It makes you want to go out and make things right before it's too late.

But I don't think it's going to be in politics that I make a difference—at least not in this lifetime (or maybe it's just not in this decade—then we'll see).

I recently received a copy of a book called *Many Lives, Many Masters* which talks about the work we're meant to do in this life, on this planet. And it's as if someone was sending me a message with that book. That you go when you've finished the task you had to do here. It's as if someone was telling me that you had finished what you had to do here, which was to help me to feel/be whole again so we could "make a difference." And since I was going to be okay—financially and emotionally—you decided it was time for you to go. I'm not saying I agree with your timing—in fact, I don't. But I do think I understand.

Jim Oleske, who is struggling more than ever to save all the babies with AIDS, sent me a lovely note when he heard about your death. He was so gracious and kind in acknowledging how much we had helped him with his work with the children. The interesting thing is by sharing his message, we've reached out again and helped people anew.

We always loved creating our holiday messages together. Last year I had to do it alone, but I know you would have liked what I did with Jim's note:

December 15, 1991

Dearest Friends,

When my beautiful beloved Norman died, I received a note from a man who, in his own way, is even more beautiful and wonderful than my Normy—Dr. James Oleske, one of the first pediatricians to discover, and fight, AIDS in babies.

We made a movie about Dr. Oleske for CBS and, as a result, he received a grant of over $2,000,000 to carry on his work. When Norman heard about that, he called me, crying like a baby because we'd helped make that happen.

In his note to me Jim wrote, "I never realized the major impact that Brooks-Field's Littlest Victims *would have on my program to care for children with AIDS. Because it was committed to telling a story many did not want to hear, and you and Norman made sure it was done with truth and clarity, a countess was moved to help. I've enclosed a story which reflects our work in Newark and I think Norman would have liked. Norman and you have helped me save not a few 'starfish.' "*

The story he enclosed goes like this:

As the old man walked the beach at dawn, he noticed a young woman ahead of him picking up starfish and flinging them into the sea. Finally catching up with the youth, he asked her why she was doing this. The answer was that the stranded starfish would die if left until the morning sun.

"But the beach goes on for miles and there are millions of starfish," countered the old man. "How can your effort make any difference?"

The young woman looked at the starfish in her hand and threw it safely into the waves. "It makes a difference to this one," she said.

Let's take this year—and all the years to come—to make a difference. I wish you a healthy and a happy New Year. I love you all.

I got a lot of responses to that holiday greeting. One letter was from Joyce Aysta. Remember her? Our art director on "The Day My Kid Went Punk." She said she'd been having a lousy year. Work was hard to find, she was feeling depressed. And then the greeting arrived and she realized she'd spent a lot of the year fixing up a place for a homeless young man and his mother to live in. And Jim's story brought home to her the fact that she had made a difference this last year. That it hadn't been such a bad year after all.

So many of the things you and I have done in our years together have brought that kind of a response. I'm going to put the letters I got when you died into an album for Adam—to remind him always of the kind of man his grandfather was. I want to have it bound like our wedding album—with your picture on the cover and the inscription will read "And this is my beloved."

Paris, May 22, 1992

Normy,

It's summer in Paris—without it ever having been spring. It just went from winter-clothes weather to temperatures in the 80s and higher in the sun at the sidewalk cafes.

Is there anything more romantic than Paris in the summer? The balmy breeze, the golden lights framed against a velvet sky with twinkling stars. The other night there was the sliver of a new moon glittering in a baby blue sky and like the good, superstitious Russian that I am, I made a wish. But wishing you could be here with me is no longer something I can ask for.

Gabriella Ranucci came to Paris the other day. I took her and her friend to dinner at the Grand Vefour on the recommendation of Christopher Plummer. It's one of his favorite restaurants—very baroque and pricey, but nice atmosphere and they loved it. It was the least I could do. After all, she had been such a gracious hostess when we stayed at her magnificent villa in Formia with Carlo and Titti in the summer of '88.

I remember that trip, my darling. How you kvelled, sitting on that 100-foot-plus sailing sloop that Carlo had rented—less than a year after having artificial valves put into your heart. And how many times you commented that the previous August you never would have imagined that you'd be sailing the Mediterranean to Palinuro. (In the summer of '87 we were shooting a movie up in Lake Arrowhead and you were having trouble breathing.)

And remember Bonny Dore and Sandy Astor's wedding five years ago (it hardly seems possible it's been that long) at the Moulin de Mougins? They were here for a few days on their way down to celebrate their anniversary and attend the Cannes Film Festival—and again on their way back home. They left this morning, after we talked a lot about you.

Last night I told Bonnie about this book I'm writing and gave her the reprint from the temple newsletter of the first letter I wrote to you. The one entitled: "A Letter to My Darling Husband on the First Anniversary of His Death." She melted into tears and came to me and said, "If you don't finish this book, I'll never speak to you again."

She's been in New Zealand, by the way, making a movie with Jon Voight about the "Rainbow Warrior." Only they were in Auckland, as is Tom Cotter with the last season of *The Ray Bradbury Theater*. He wrote me the nicest note about his memories of our visit with him in Scotland the summer before you passed away. I must tell him once again how much that trip meant to you. Even though, by then, that idiot doctor (I have a mental block about his name) had scared you half to death. I'm convinced if that had not happened—you might still be here today.

You see, I've formulated this theory. You might not buy into it—and Philip says blood clots don't travel that way. But that's not what I heard—and other doctors I've mentioned it to have thought my theory has some legs.

And yes, I know you had developed an occlusion in one of your bypasses sometime in the summer of '90. It showed up in the October angiogram, and the doctors said it had probably occurred three or four months earlier. Thinking back on it now, I think I can pinpoint the exact day.

We had driven up to Jasper from Edmonton for the Canada Day holiday weekend. It was June 30th. I know because that was the day my cousin Bob died. When we came back to the hotel after dinner that night—the message was waiting for us, and you, especially, were so upset.

I remember we had arrived early in the afternoon, carried our bags up the one flight of stairs to our room and started out for a walk. Two blocks from the hotel you stopped and complained of having a chest pain. God, Normy, I wish now that I had stopped to think how bad it must have been, because you never complain. I wish we had gotten our bags and left then and there. Maybe the altitude was too high, the air too thin.

I guess Dr. Charuzi's right. When I told him I was surprised by your death, that I hadn't suspected your condition was that serious, he said I didn't want to know...and that you hadn't wanted to know, either. And at first I denied that, too. But he must be right because to this day when someone says to me, "Well, Norman had such a bad heart..." or "He was so sick," I look at them like they're nuts—and wonder, who are they talking about? They can't mean you! Because they're painting a picture of a sick, fragile old man—and I'm remembering my beautiful, strong, gorgeous husband, who was ever the adventurous optimist.

Like in January of '90, when we were considering going to work in New Zealand and I asked how you felt about that: if it concerned you, if you were afraid to go so far away from home, from the doctors you trusted, because after your valve operation in 1987, things had become a little more complex. You shook your head, smiled at me and said, "Fernie, I'm not going to sit in the living room waiting to die."

And I recall how every day in New Zealand you'd walk out on the balcony, look at the bay of Wellington and say, "I can breathe here!" You felt so much better down there—where the air is clean and the pollution minimal—and I remembered the first time you ever said to me that you felt differently because of the air. It was in Calgary years earlier when I was doing *Mr. Wizard's World*, and I said, "Let's move," but you weren't ready for that. And now I sit and wonder how much of it you were saying and doing, just for me.

So that day in Jasper in the summer of '90 when you got the chest pain, I didn't get too upset. I told you to sit down (wasn't it lucky there was a bench right there?), I'd get the car and we could sight-see in comfort. I didn't think it was anything serious. Just a little angina. My father had lived a lot of years with that. So had my aunt—and I was sure their hearts had been much sicker than yours. And now I think it's possible you got the occlusion right then and there. Or perhaps walking in the high altitude simply made you aware of it.

Anyway, that fall in the hospital, after the angiogram had diagnosed the blockage, and I was debating with your doctors whether or not to try to dissolve it with medication, Dr. Buchbinder told me how lucky we had been that you hadn't had a fatal heart attack when that new blockage first occurred! (And I thanked God silently that you didn't, especially on that quiet street in Jasper.) Buchbinder continued to stress that we'd had our miracle then—you had been spared. He felt it would be a mistake to go pushing our luck. He didn't think we should go looking for another miracle by trying to dissolve the new clot now. There were too many risks. I agreed, figuring we—actually, you—had already had more than your share of miracles. After all, heart attack in '72, quadruple bypass in '80, two artificial valves in '87— how much more could your poor body withstand?

But Charuzi was gung ho, and you, ever the optimist, wanted to try for another miracle yet again. So, even though it was way past 10 p.m., they began prepping you for surgery, and I was still living this day that felt like it would never end!

As I walked back toward the lobby to wait again—with the bleak prognosis of the doctor's words ringing in my ears—my mind reviewed the events of the past few days.

Because of your artificial valves, they needed to wean you off one blood-thinning medication and put you on another before they did the angiogram. So, we'd been in the hospital for a couple of days. Me with my computer, rewriting scripts, going home to fax and receive pages! And you, sort of happy you were finally going to know what was wrong.

At last, this morning, you were ready for the procedure, and I was scared. I couldn't understand why we needed to go through with another angiogram. It would be the third one in 10 years. After all, the purpose of the procedure is to give a road map for open-heart surgery, and you had already said you didn't want any more operations. And we'd been to a specialist in New York, who said that with whatever was going on in your system—with your history and medical profile—your chances of surviving surgery were the same as surviving without it! It's an invasive procedure and so many things can go wrong. And suddenly you can find yourself in the middle of a medical nightmare, like so many people we've known.

I remembered the woman Bobbi and I met when you were in intensive care after your valve surgery in '87. Her husband was on the road to recovery and had been moved out of the ICU—and then had complained of feeling nauseous. No one paid attention, and he threw up, aspirated his own vomit and burned the lining of his lungs, and things went downhill from there, like in the Dyan Cannon film (*Such Good Friends* was the title, I think), where her husband goes in for a hangnail, or something silly like that, and winds up dying. But this was no movie. Bobbi and I were sitting in the waiting area outside ICU hearing about a real medical nightmare that was far worse than that.

That woman's husband was back in intensive care, practically in a coma, in critical condition, and it had been going on for weeks. And I remembered thinking then, how could you and I survive—emotionally, financially—if anything like that happened to us?

My mind came back to the present, and I wondered if trying to dissolve this clot tonight was going to take me down the path that woman had walked then.

I was alone in the lobby now, and the hour was closing in on midnight as my thoughts drifted back to the events of earlier that day. I remembered your brother Philip, who's always by your side during all your procedures and visibly reduces your blood pressure with his presence, coming out an hour later after accompanying you into the operating room for the angiogram and telling us they hadn't been able to get into an artery yet. The veins in your groin were so fragile they would probably have to go in through the arm—a procedure they they didn't do very frequently at Cedars. And much later, in intensive care, they were explaining to us that there was blockage in one of the four bypasses (which sounded like pretty good odds to me—three out of the four were still good) and you were not a candidate for surgery (now I can't remember if they told us why), but they could try to dissolve the clot with medication. But there were no odds they could give us that it would work, and there could be serious complications. Dr. Charuzi was for it, while Dr. Buchbinder was more conservative—and, of course, it was your decision. They had left the arm vein open so they could get back in. You opted to try, and I had to respect your decision. Now here it was, the middle of the night, and they were prepping you for the procedure...and, my God, how I was afraid.

And then suddenly they were back—the two doctors standing in front of me, guiding me to your bedside in intensive care—and it was well past midnight. They were telling us they had discussed it some more, and the risks outweighed the benefits. You had been through too much that day; it was too iffy. You could hemorrhage, you could get an infection. They would stitch up the vein for easy access, and in a couple of weeks, when you were stronger, you could come back.

How relieved I was. I just wanted to get out of there as quickly as possible—to have this nightmare come to an end. To take you home and never go near another hospital again.

It took another couple of days to get you weaned from one medication back to your regular prescription, and now you were more like your old self. The valves, which had you worried, were okay—and your frame of mind seemed to be better.

And I don't remember discussing it very much between us, but then we were sitting in Charuzi's office days later and you were saying you had decided not to try to go back in to dissolve the clot. He didn't approve, but I agreed with your decision. I had to get back to work and I wanted you as far away from hospitals as I could get you. I was so afraid of all the things that could go wrong—and was so sure you could live for another 20 years if we just took care of you and kept you away from stress. Since we were out of "development" and I had a regular job, why couldn't this be the time of our lives when "the best is yet to be"?

Of course, when I used to say my father lived a long time with angina—I forgot that you had had your first heart attack 20 years ago! In 1972. I remember you told me you drove yourself to the hospital that time—after arranging to meet your doctor there because you knew you were having one and realized staying in control would keep you alive!

And I remember the night in June of 1980 when you came back from the summer Consumer Electronics Show in Chicago. I had come back a couple of days earlier for a meeting with my boss, Norman Lear, leaving you with the suitcases. You came home close to midnight, looking rather pale—but I thought it was normal fatigue from the trip. And we went to sleep and you never said a thing!

For some reason I had told my secretary I wouldn't be in the next day because something told me I needed to spend it with you. The next morning you got up and said very casually that you were going to call Dr. Kuhn because you'd had some chest pains and you wanted to go in for a test. Only later—much later—did you tell me that you had had such severe pains you'd barely made it down the airport concourse to the plane; you'd only been carrying a book and that was an enormous effort. You said you'd spent the whole trip just praying to God you'd make it home! (At the time, I was reading *Heartsounds*, which I wound up producing four years later. An airport scene just like the one you lived through is in the book!)

But I didn't know all that when we went to your doctor at the end of the day and you were on the treadmill and told me you were having the same pains. I, like a dummy, said, "Good," because that way they'd be able to diagnose it. (Unlike when you go to the dentist and the toothache has gone away.) I still thought he'd tell you the usual about losing weight and getting some exercise.

Surprise, surprise. Kuhn sat us down in his office and said he was usually very conservative about such things, but he was 99-percent certain that you'd need bypass surgery. And we asked, "What's the alternative?" "Sudden death," he replied, and elaborated from there.

Then you, my dear, sweet husband, tried to tell him that you wanted to wait until after my birthday because we had chartered John Davidson's yacht for a weekend cruise to Catalina for a double celebration (it was my mother's birthday, too). As you talked, I envisioned having to call a helicopter in the middle of the festivities to airlift you back to the hospital. So, I said we'd forgo the cruise and would celebrate my birthday later (which we did in the sixth-floor lobby at Cedars). I still haven't been to Catalina.

Dr. Kuhn told us since it was Thursday evening, he wouldn't put you into the hospital till Sunday because they wouldn't do anything till Monday, anyway. But he cautioned that, unlike other times when he told you to walk and exercise, he didn't want you to do anything at all. No exertion, no stress or strain. And we went home that night—just the two of us—holding each other very tight and contemplated the unthinkable.

God, what a night that was! The next morning, Dr. Kuhn called and said he was checking you into the hospital right away so you could have immediate attention should anything happen.

It was the best thing he could have done for us—because instead of a brooding, solitary weekend of "good-bye," it became a party. Everyone came by the hospital, all the well-wishers. I told the world, and got

them to call because I knew it would mean a lot to you.
So, Bea Arthur called and Jerry Stiller and Anne Meara
from New York, and all our friends (and you kept a list,
which I still have). You went into that operation on a real
high—with the attitude that this surgery was going to
make you well, give you a new lease on life. And they
told us bypasses last at least 10 years. And you liked
those numbers, and said you would resort to more than
open-heart surgery to have a guarantee of 10 more years
with me. And it was almost 10 years to the day when the
new occlusion occurred!

The valves seven years later were a different story.
The doctors had given us a lot of hope with the bypass
surgery. The odds were clearly in our favor. This time,
you didn't know, but the doctors were painting a very
bleak picture. The odds had gone way down. But I had
learned a valuable lesson from you. You always told me
there's no use worrying in advance about something that
might not happen. So, although the thought was always
in the back of my head, I really didn't torture myself
with the thought that something might go wrong. And
every day, I went back home to change clothes. I'd
watched enough TV and movies to know that bad things
happen in hospitals at night, so I just slept in the sixth-
floor lobby because they don't put cots for wives into the
ICU. I refused to think about what it would be like if
something went wrong and you didn't return home with
me.

The day after the valve operation you developed some respiratory problems and as night fell, you were having more trouble breathing. It was Thanksgiving and towards dawn on Friday morning, when I went to look in on you as I did every couple of hours all through the night and day, I overheard a conversation between the two ICU doctors changing shifts.

They were looking at your chart and the doctor coming on was reviewing the medication that had been prescribed for you. "Is that what you're giving him?" he asked. And the outgoing doctor nodded, and the incoming doctor said, "Well, it's not what I would give him, but as long as that's what was prescribed, we'll continue the medication." I blew my stack.

I called Dr. Kuhn, your personal physician for more than 20 years, and demanded to know just who was in charge of this case, and how was the intensive care staff supposed to know about you—not just a body in a bed—your history, your special needs. Within a couple of hours he was there with the surgeon and a respiratory specialist Philip recommended. Soon, you were beginning to breathe more easily—and so was I.

The doctors had been most concerned that your heart might not respond well when they took you off the machines after this surgery, but you surprised them as I knew you would. I was convinced that your heart would see the new valves and say, "Lemme at 'em!" Which is exactly what it did. The doctors were astounded. But the recovery was slower this time. And the psychological impact was greater. I empathized with you. I could imagine how invasive it must be to have foreign objects in your heart. This had truly been "open-heart" surgery. And now we could hear the "click, click, click" of your artificial valves. Scary and reassuring at the same time. (Remember how we laughed when you got your "life-time warranty" for the valves in the mail?)

But now life became a little more complicated for you. Not only did you have to take more medication daily, you had to have your blood checked every four to six weeks—wherever we might be—to make sure it wasn't coagulating and clogging the valves.

That's why when you came back from Jasper and went to have your blood checked, what that young doctor did to you was unforgivable. I didn't go with you that day—and how I wish I had. The story you told me!

It must have been a Wednesday because Kuhn and Cristal weren't in, so you were seen by their junior partner. He was taking your blood to check it and asked how you were feeling. So you told him you'd had some severe chest pains when we were in the Canadian Rockies. And this genius who calls himself a doctor said, "Well, you know they're having problems with the valves." You asked what kind of problems. And that unthinking jerk said, matter-of-factly, "They're defective." When you asked what the recourse might be, he said simply, "Surgery."

You came home that night and I had never seen you so pale and so upset. You were scared to death.

The next day, I was there when you called him for the results of the blood test—and to tell him you had looked up the name and make of your valves, and he had the unmitigated gall to say, "Oh, I made a mistake—you don't have the defective ones!" I flew into a rage. That insensitive clod had not even had the decency—or the good sense—to call you as soon as he found that out. To reassure you and apologize, and set your mind at ease! (And a doctor is supposed to heal! Apparently compassion, sensitivity and caring are not prerequisites for a medical degree these days.)

At least I was able to let Kuhn know exactly what I thought of his junior partner when I had him banned from your case. And Kuhn, at least, had the decency to apologize that someone in his office had caused us such distress.

But you never recovered from the effects of that callousness. Had I been there with you when you went in for your test, I could have relieved your anguish. We knew about the company that was having trouble with their valves. It had been on the news and in the papers, and we knew they were not the valves you had—which were St. Jude's. You had just forgotten that. But you would think that someone who calls himself a doctor would have handled the situation more delicately. And that any doctor's office in general would have taken the time and trouble to find out if any of their patients had the defective valves implanted, and would have called them in to discuss the ramifications and the alternatives. Apparently not.

You were so stunned and troubled by what he had said that from that moment on, you thought your pains and problems and the changes you were sensing in your chest, stemmed from the valves. It didn't matter anymore that you knew the problem wasn't with the St. Jude valves.

Every time you felt a twinge, you thought it was the valves malfunctioning. You spent all the next months—until the angiogram proved otherwise—worrying, counting "clicks" and being afraid.

That's why you wanted to, agreed to take the angiogram. Not because you would have agreed to more surgery, but because you had to know if the valves were okay.

And it turned out they were fine. And frankly, when they told us there was blockage in only one of the four bypasses, I thought you were home free. But I think that because the angiogram was so traumatic for your system (because they'd had such a hard time trying to get into the leg artery—finally having to switch to the arm) that it caused a blood clot.

And that's what the excruciating pain was that you felt in your groin about a month later in Toronto—even though they couldn't find traces of a clot anywhere. I think that clot traveled around and finally lodged in another artery the night you died. And I think if that doctor in L.A. hadn't scared you to death about the valves, you would have taken the other tests but not the angiogram—because you wouldn't have been questioning if the valves were really okay. And maybe another clot wouldn't have formed, and maybe you would still be alive today.

You see, I think your death was a mistake. It wasn't time. You could have lived with blockage in one out of four bypasses. There were ancillary vessels that had taken over. Something happened that wasn't supposed to. You were not meant to die when you did.

The Lonely Beach

To dream and to grow old,
And to have the winter of life
Embrace you in its coldness.
The years and dreams have disappeared
Like the children from the autumn beaches.
Our lives loom empty, like the sands around us,
The crashing waves echo youth's exuberance
And the wind reminds us of life's fleeting moments
Too swift to hold, too strong to be ignored.
Oh, how I long to bring back the Summer
With the warmth of its summer sun.
Or recapture Spring,
With its promise of things to come.
Yet, Autumn is here and with it the cold,
lonely, desolate days.
Yes. Autumn is here and Winter will come.

Paris, May 31, 1992

My darling,

I went to London this weekend. Traveling by myself is getting harder, more painful. I sit in the cab and you're not sitting next to me and the ache starts deep in my gut and rises inside me and tears fill my eyes and I talk to you and the floodwaters of my emotions overwhelm me and I wonder how I can bear the agony.

I tell myself that's why I was so stupid and got myself into real hot water with French customs the other day. You would really have been annoyed with me, but then if you'd been with me, I probably wouldn't have done such an asinine thing.

I had bought a couple of really expensive items when I was in Cannes for the biannual television market. I was planning to take them with me this weekend—but then the weather turned bad. It was raining in Paris, and rain was forecast for London, and I no longer had a raincoat. (I gave my old one—the one we bought together at Burberry's when we were in London with our mothers back in 1978—to someone who was collecting clothes for the Yugoslavian refugees. Oh yes, you don't know that Yugoslavia is no more. There's been a civil war there for well over a year. Dubrovnick—all those lovely places we talked of visiting—the cities where Branka's family live—they're all under siege. It's like Beirut—and the history books will report that "the Western Powers fiddled while the rest of the world burned.")

Anyway, since I didn't have a raincoat, I decided not to take this expensive Dior jacket and leather bag only to get them ruined in the rain. But I still wanted to process the customs tax rebate since that's what I had planned to do. And, dummy that I am, when they asked to see the items, I tried to bluff my way through instead of simply saying I didn't have them with me and getting the rebate on my next trip, which was only two weeks away! Well, they nailed me! They caught me lying, red-handed. I had to pay a fine—and lost the rebate too. Worst of all, I felt so stupid for having tried to pull a dumb stunt like that.

But, it's only money. When you've lost someone you love, it's funny how things take on a totally different perspective. Like when our post office lost a whole week's worth of mail en route from L.A. to Toronto the month after you died. (Our mail service wanted to do me a favor and save money by not using Fed Ex. Never again.)

And I was really broken up about the lost package— because it was shortly after your death and I'm sure there were letters from friends that would have meant a lot to me. But when I measured that loss against the one of losing you—it was hard to get really excited about it. In fact, it's hard to get excited about a lot of things that bothered the hell out of me when you were still here.

Like flying. As you know, the older I got—the more I was afraid of flying. I think it's because you begin to cling to life the closer you get to the time of your death.

So I was really surprised when on my first flight after you passed away, I was as calm as I could be. And I suddenly knew why. Because it didn't matter anymore if something happened. Without you, there was no reason to cling to life. If I died, so be it.

A lot of the time when I travel now I feel a little like a zombie. I do the things I know I need to do—but I do them by rote. My head is someplace else.

And, my God, Normy, the money! The different currencies—I hate them! They're overwhelming without you there to do the instant arithmetic that you used to do so quickly in your head. Now, not only do I have to remember to take the tickets, get cash for the trip, cancel the newspapers, arrange for transportation, all the things you used to take care of—but converting the currencies, that's the real pain! So, I rarely bother. If I run out of money before my time comes—I'm sure someone will take me in.

Although I may not be going so quickly. While I'm still smoking (even buying my own occasionally), which would upset you, you'd be proud of me because I've been going to a gym almost every day. Bonny Dore inspired and motivated me to go when she and Sandy were here. (She was in a bad automobile accident so she's had to work out for her back every day for almost a year).

The other day Simon saw me taking a cigarette and said, "Fernanda, Norman would be really upset." I laughed and agreed that you must be really ticked at me. And

Simon said you were probably also angry with him because he's not stopping me. I'm sure that's true. But I'll have to stop myself. Just like I have to be the one who makes me lose some weight.

But, you see, even though it's gotten better on the job, I'm still under a lot of stress in my life without you.

Last winter, when things came to a head at work, it got so stressful that I woke up one morning and couldn't move. My back had locked on me from the tension. I remembered you told me about when you spent 13 weeks flat on your back and the doctor told you, whatever you're in—get out of it.

And I realized how scary it can be not to be able to move and to be alone. I thought of all the disabled people we worked with and realized how very courageous they are. It is very scary not to be able to move or control things in your own environment.

Somehow I managed to get out of bed and get myself dressed. Even though my "distant cousin," Micheline, was out of town, her whole family are doctors, so I called and got some pills that helped me. They also prescribed rest—but I couldn't do that. It was a Friday and on Sunday my first house guests, Joann, your successor as president of the temple, and her new husband, Yossi, were arriving and I was having a party. The first time I would be entertaining since your death.

Paris was healing my soul at that time. I was ready to entertain. That was a milestone, Normy. In Toronto I had had a very nice apartment. You would have liked that one. And when I first took it, I immediately thought, as we always did, "great place for a party." It was getting to be that wherever we hung our hats was "home"—even a hotel suite we might be in for only a couple of weeks.

However, just like that January of 1991 in New York, when I kept talking about having a party in our suite on January 4 or 5, I couldn't bring myself to call anybody. I couldn't entertain in Toronto, either. Not yet. It was too soon. It was admitting that you would not be coming back. That I had to make a home alone. I couldn't bring myself to do that.

But last February in Paris, I was ready. I was energized. Joann said how happy she was to see me in this environment. And since then, I've had a couple of other get-togethers. "Salons" as Adele Scheele described the brunch I had while she was here, remembering those we used to have on our gigantic deck on Tahiti Way.

However, it's getting harder, Normy, not easier. Because I have no roots, because I don't know where I belong, don't know where to make a life, because no place seems tolerable without you.

Our mothers were right. They said there are days when the phone doesn't even ring. And you were right about kids—they only find the number when they need something. It seems being in Paris makes it harder for people to think of calling just to say hello, even though it's not that expensive. Yet this environment is more soothing, more civilized. I'm not complaining—you know how I hate the phone—I'm just commenting on reality, telling it like it is. I've always grounded myself in a person, in a relationship, in someone I love. I was grounded in you! Now where and when will I find out where I belong?

Paris, June 3, 1992

Normy,

Alopecia areata. I think I have it. And I don't want it. Getting old, and being without you is bad enough—being bald to boot is simply not acceptable.

They say you can get it from trauma, like the loss of a loved one. Normy, if you've charmed them up there like you charmed everyone down here, you have to fix this. I definitely don't want to lose my hair.

I also think it could be from my hypothyroidism, or the increased dose of hormones I'm taking. I'm going to write Philip and Paul Rudnick about that. Meanwhile I've already cut down on the medications because given the choice between osteoporosis (which I don't have) and being bald (which I am getting), I'll take the former.

So far, all the doctors who have seen me lately—eye doctor, dentist, Philip, Paul—have said I have the organs, veins, etc., of someone 15 years younger. Now all I have to do is get the figure and the face in shape to match. Then what? I don't know, but it's a start—a goal to reach for. Not having any hair is not part of that picture!

It's funny how things connect in life. As you know, I've been complaining that my hair was getting thinner for a lot of years and made you promise to give me a hair transplant for my 60th birthday. (Which I may still have to give myself when that day comes along!)

I stayed blonde for a while after you died, but you know I never felt like one. I did it because you liked it.

But the older I got, the more I disliked it. Because it made me look like my mother and my aunt, and all the old ladies you see in those neighborhood beauty shops and even *chi-chi* places like Alexandre in Paris—where the hairdressers have grown old with their clientele and the hip crowd has gone elsewhere.

Anyway, I thought part of the hair loss might be due to torturing my hair with coloring it these many years. And, of course, going back to being a brunette, which I'd also been contemplating for a while, wasn't going to help that. With my hair a light blonde, the gray wouldn't show sometimes for six to eight weeks—dark hair would be much more revealing. But the decision was taken out of my hands.

In trying to find a color I liked, this place I was going to in Toronto did something one day that first turned my hair sort of pink. Of course I hated that, so I told my secretary to get me some darker coloring without any ammonia or peroxide and I would do it myself.

I was going to New York for the weekend to attend Lisa Korn's wedding (Larry Keith's daughter, remember her?). I changed my reservation to a slightly later flight, got up early and went to work on my hair. Only the color Keitha got wasn't dark enough. I dried it and stared.

My hair had turned a sort of orange color—something like your sister Natalie's, or Lucille Ball's, if you will. It was a pretty enough color, but it looked awful on me! Well, I wasn't about to go to the wedding looking like that! But, I also had a plane to catch. So, I threw on my clothes and headed to the airport, with no make-up, orange hair, and the determination to fix it as soon as I landed.

Of course, as luck would have it, I ran into my boss Sonny Grosso at the airport, and we sat next to each other on the plane. So here's this poor man who hates flying anyway, sitting next to this ludicrous apparition looking a lot like a witch decked out for Halloween. He, of course, had the good grace not to say anything—or maybe he couldn't quite figure out what was wrong. But I'm sure he spent the whole flight feeling nauseous and wondering what it was about me that made me look so strange!

Anyway, as soon as I got off the plane I made a bee-line for the nearest drugstore and got the darkest brown color I could get—and that turned my hair "eggplant black"! But it was time to leave for the wedding—and twice in one day is probably as much as even "young" hair can take. The funny thing was that everybody loved my "new look." They said it made me look younger and I, of course, just felt like I was back to being me.

More and more I see my mother in me—and I don't want that. I know she was a beautiful woman, and I could do a lot worse than growing old like she did. But I want to be *me* and sometimes I feel she's invading my mind, my body and my life.

I see her gestures in mine, her shadow in the way I walk and do something. When I had dinner with Julie that night in Boston, at one point he told me I reminded him of my mother. You know me and my occasional clairvoyance—I had known at some point he was going to say that to me! And I didn't want to remind him of her.

I remember the times she complained about growing old and I was not properly sympathetic. I told her not to worry about the wrinkles—that we loved her and couldn't see them. She would threaten that it was going to happen to me. I feel like somehow this is her revenge. She's getting even with me, showing me what it feels like to be getting old...alone.

It's true that I understand a lot of things better now—the things she must have gone through. I remember back to when she took me to Italy when I was a pretty teenager, and all the men who used to "court and flirt" with her, were now doing it with me! She was still a young woman, but suddenly they had eyes only for me. I never realized that until now. She and I used to philosophize about a lot of things when I was a teenager, but we never talked about that. I guess that was too hard to discuss, too hard to come to grips with. So, yes, mother, I know what that feels like now. It is happening to me!

So, about the hair loss. I knew I was in trouble one day when, while washing my hair in the shower of my mirrored Parisian bathroom, I saw bald spots in too many places!

My heart sank to my toes and did a flip flop. Then I went into a deep depression. Finally, I remembered a recent article from the *International Herald Tribune* that I had cut out to take back to L.A. It was titled "Sudden Baldness: Experts Baffled."

I had only heard of alopecia once before when my then-boss Rod Parker wrote about a character who had it for an episode of *The Nancy Walker Show*.

The article says that by age 50, one person in 100 will have experienced this "capricious condition." Not much consolation there. And it's on the increase, some experts claim, because of dirt, pollution, modern-day stress, etc.

The hairdresser I had gone to at Alexandre told me of some pills they sell in Switzerland. They contain minoxidil, but he said you need a 3-percent solution to have any effect.

So, I went to a dermatologist to find out about my hair and my nails (they're nonexistent because of the vertical ridges that keep splitting, and no one seems to have figured that out yet either) and she's prescribed a French product with minoxidil in it, but I didn't realize until later it was only a 2-percent solution.

As the article says, "Tests with minoxidil...show that it can often foster hair growth in *alopecia areata* as well... But higher concentrations are needed than are now being marketed..." (or prescribed, they should have added). So what good is using it?

It's such a funny world we live in. Like, you're dying of an incurable disease, there's an experimental drug that could save your life, but you can't get it, because it could kill you. Huh?

Paris, June 6, 1992

God, Normy, it's another weekend again. A holiday one at that—three days!

I wake up on a Saturday morning now and the ache overtakes me. Yes, there are things to do, errands to run, but it's a day we would have spent together—holding, kissing, touching. The longing starts and doesn't go away.

Sometimes you'd like to put your arms around a warm body—make love to another human being—and then you look around and think, who? Who exudes the warmth, the heart, the soul, the sensuality, the passion that would allow me to open up to them? That would make me want to love them, and lose myself in them? And I walk the streets and look at the faces and wonder if ever again there will be anyone to hold, to love. I think how many people there are who don't have that—who may never have had that. I remember the conversations we had about many of our friends. You would comment about how lonely you thought they were. You were always so sensitive to that—and would make a point of calling someone just to say hello, or to include them in our plans.

It's hard for me to imagine living without loving someone ever again. I don't mean friends or family or a one-night stand. I mean someone you care about. It's so important—really what life is all about. I still have a lot of love to give.

It's now June 8th...

I went to the Rodin Museum on Sunday. It was a beautiful day. The sky was a vibrant blue, with puffy white clouds sprinkled here and there. It looked like someone had thrown a bag of cotton balls into the air. And it was warm—but not too warm. Just a perfect day.

The tourists and the few natives that were left in town were out in droves. Everyone seemed to be in couples—and I thought about how bitter some of my friends are about that. But I didn't feel that way that day. It's okay to go to a museum by yourself—or a play or a movie. Because a good movie is a good movie—even if you see it by yourself.

It's the beauty of a bright, clear day or the glow of a golden sunset or the soaring flight of a bird. Those are the things that are hard to take alone. It's the fleeting beauty of life and this world of ours—that we're destroying so rapidly, and so efficiently, but which still has incredibly beautiful moments that you want to share with someone you love.

It's not being able to share the beauty that really brings the pain.

You know there's an entire alcove of Rodin designs and sketches that could easily be considered hard porn. A man bending over, exposing (all of his) rear. A woman, legs apart, touching herself. I noticed they didn't make those sketches into postcards. I think you'd be arrested by the FBI if you tried to send them through the mail. If more people knew about that section—especially the tourists—the museum would probably do even more business than they're doing these days.

The garden is gorgeous. You would have had a field day with your camera. On one side of the villa, the golden dome of the Invalides stands framed between conical-shaped trees. On the other side, the famed "Thinker" sits high on his perch, while the dome and the Eiffel Tower provide a backdrop to the garden full of green bushes and roses of every size, shape and color. Truly breath-taking and just a very short walk from my beautiful apartment.

I seem to have gotten my head together at least as far as the gym is concerned. I've been going every single day and have already dropped a whole bathing-suit size! Can you imagine? And it's just been a few weeks. (Next will be the dieting!)

I pass the time on the treadmill at the gym, finding counterparts for the regulars in my head: There's one thin, intense young man—he's Peewee Herman. Another man looks like Ted Danson, and there's a woman who reminds me of Dorothea Petrie.

And then I look to see if anyone appeals. There are a couple of nice-looking men, the right age, in good shape, who seemed interesting at first. I watched them for a few days. They're there every morning—and then one day I suddenly realized they're together. They must be gay!

That's the way it is these days, Normy. The whole world is either married or gay—or both.

Norman, my love,

I met Pam and Jack Wishard here on Friday. They came to help me celebrate my birthday and it's been a wonderful three days.

The pain didn't start until this morning—as I began to pack. Alone again—getting ready to leave this place and go somewhere else.

The car that would take me to Naples wasn't coming till after lunch, so when I finished packing I went down to the "beach"—a concrete platform carved out of the rock with lounge chairs and a bar overlooking one of the most beautiful, tiny harbors and fishing villages in the world. (Don't know how much fishing they really do these days—except for tourists, that is.)

We stopped here on the sloop with Carlo and Titti a few years ago—remember? We didn't get off then because the water had been too dirty and we were heading farther south. This time the water is crystal clear. But occasionally, early in the morning, you get the smell of sewage and have to ask yourself, "If not in the ocean, where would it go?"

I think I was here many years ago with my mother, maybe even while my father was still alive. I remember taking a drive along the Amalfi coast, but this is the first time I've actually stayed. Pam and Jack picked it and I was glad they did. It's not a place I would ever come to by myself.

The San Pietro is reputed to be one of the best hotels in the world. It is certainly one of the most beautiful. Nestled into the side of a cliff, it is barely visible as you approach it. But once you enter its spacious lobby/bar area you see the little town of Positano framed in the arched windows and at night it sparkles like a jewel.

Last night the hotel hosted a big party in honor of Saint Peter (San Pietro)—which it does annually. It was like a bar mitzvah, or an Italian wedding, complete with fireworks and what had to be the local "godfather" presiding on the terrace over the entire scene. You would have loved it. It was really straight out of one of Mario Puzo's epics. The faces would have been a credit to "central casting" and were the personification of any one of Francis Ford Coppola's dreams.

And I got picked up by a local guy last night. He tried at least. He was very sweet, but he wasn't my type. It's happened before—once in Toronto, twice in Cannes, and now in Positano. Unfortunately, not one of them was the man of my dreams!

Gloria says I've had the love of my life. Now I should go for the CEO. She also says there are signals a woman sends out when she's available, and she says I'm not sending out those signals. Easy for her to say.

First of all, what she doesn't realize is, the CEO is probably looking for—or more likely already has—someone 20 or 30 years younger than he is. Second of all, how do I change my standards this late in the game? I've never gone out for money, God knows. I've always had to be "in love," or at least "intrigued" by something, someone.

As I always told you, and how you loved to hear it, all my life I was looking for a fairytale life, a '40s movie like the ones I used to see with my mother when I was a little girl, where the prince and princess live happily ever after. That never necessarily meant money as far as I was concerned. It really meant "loved happily ever after." And I found that with you. We had our '40s movie. You were my knight in shining armor—my beautiful, loving, caring prince.

You're a tough act to follow, my darling, and who's going to want me, love me, pursue me, the way you did?

As for me sending out signals, in spite of those four aborted attempts, I think I forgot how to do that a long time ago. Or maybe it's that I always responded to someone else's signal. Maybe someone else has to be the first one to start flirting, to hold out "their hand."

Besides, I have another concern—something else that bothers me. If there is an afterlife, a place where we all meet again, who goes with whom?

I mean are you up there with Anita, and when I come up there is it going to be a triangle all over again? And, if I meet someone wonderful and live out the rest of my life with him—what happens when we die? I mean who'll meet me at the end of the tunnel when I walk into the light?

Oh well, you always knew I was crazy—and worried about crazy things.

Like when I still lived in New York and I told you I worried whenever I got on a plane because a lot of people had lent me things for my apartment after I separated from Konny, and how would they get them back if I was killed in a plane crash? And you suggested I put stickers on the bottom of everything saying, "This lamp belongs to so-and-so" or "Please return this chair to such and such."

I thought that was a great idea, although I never got around to doing it. But several times I did stop in at my attorney's office en route to the airport to draw up and sign a new will!

As I said, you didn't fall in love with me because I was so sane.

Normy,

Cyrielle Claire just called. She remembers you so
fondly. She said when she was having all her problems
negotiating with the production company, you gave her
great solace because you were caring and you listened. It
meant a lot to her—and you would love knowing that.
You thought she was so beautiful—and she is.

She's back in town and wants Simon and me and our
producer, Adam Haight, to come to dinner before we all
leave France, which everyone is getting ready to do. My
Parisian sojourn is coming to an end.

Yesterday, I got sick at the gym. Well, not at the
gym—on the way home, but I knew something was
wrong while I was on the treadmill.

Of course, the first thought was "heart attack!" But I
knew it wasn't anything like that. And then the stomach
pains came and the thought was "cancer!" But then I
knew it was something mundane—like a stomach virus—
which flushed through my system like Niagara Falls. At
times like that you start to think, "God, how do I deal with
a major illness alone, without your love and support?"

Not that I would have wished that on you, because
there is nothing worse, nothing more difficult than to
watch the suffering of someone you love and not be able

to do anything. But to go through something like that without the person you love by your side holding your hand…

And then you think—maybe you would end it. There would be no reason to struggle, no reason to fight. To go through that and hang on to life. By yourself. Alone.

Pam, Jack and I had long talks in Positano about where to live. L.A. is getting worse every day. There were two big earthquakes (7.4 and 6-point-something within three days) while we were in Positano. I saw one of them happen on television. I was watching CNN when it struck. Ah, the wonders of modern technology!

And they told me about seeing someone accosted by a druggie right on their street. Someone else was murdered for his car—shot in the head right in front of their gate only steps from Sunset Boulevard. And the same thing happened in front of one of our writer's houses—and he lives in the marina. Looks like it will be a while before real estate values pick up in L.A.!

I still have the Palm Desert condo. When the economy went sour, our lease/option tenant couldn't come up with the money to close the sale. He moved out without giving me any notice at all. You never liked him. I should have known your judgment of people was, as usual, better than mine.

Sometimes I wonder if I should make that my base—Palm Desert is cheaper to maintain than L.A. But I don't think it would work, even if I planned to spend my summers traveling.

I need some time at home. To move out of the office storage room I still have at Washington Place. To get rid of all the files and boxes that I just stacked in the apartment den and loft when I moved out of the office just a couple of weeks after your death and only days before getting on the plane back to Toronto.

I should redecorate the loft to make it more functional, but I still can't do that. The thought of getting rid of *your* desk, changing *your* office, rearranging the pictures *you* hung on the wall, panics me. And the thought of selling the apartment and starting anew—making a life that isn't "our life"—terrifies me.

If anything is grounding me—giving me the courage I need to go on—it's what we had, what we shared together. You not only *were*, you still are, the "wind beneath my wings." Maybe I do have to say good-bye in order to go on with my life, but what if I say good-bye and no one comes to take your place? And what, who, can fill the void you left?

Gloria sent me an article from *New York Magazine* entitled "Equal Opportunity Advertising." It shows a picture of a young man in a wheelchair and a pretty young girl in a gym. They're both in workout clothes and the commercial is for Budweiser.

Remember the response, and the resistance, we got when we first started working to encourage equal opportunity for people with disabilities, especially from the ad agencies? Looks like we've come a long way, baby. The article goes on to cite commercials and ads from companies like McDonald's, Levi Strauss and Company, IBM, Apple and many more.

Sadly, some of the people who helped forge the way with us in the early '80s are no longer here either.

Beautiful, talented, 32-inch tall Peter Riche is no longer here (or, as my aunt always put it, "has gone away"). Doris Philbrick, who was confined to a wheelchair by a stray bullet in a robbery attempt, but was so excited and proud when we gave her an opportunity to "dance" in *A Different Approach* and on stage at one of the Media Awards banquets, passed away. Lou Carillo has disappeared from the scene. And sexy, swarthy Peter Arballo, who started our whole movement by wheeling up and challenging me at a Governor's Committee meeting to do something for the disabled "instead of just exploiting us in the media," has moved out of the state. Beverly and Dennis Almacy—our wonderful Park Ranger in a wheelchair—are divorced. So are Danny and Joyce. Their girls must be quite grown up by now. Hope Yasui from the Governor's Committee on Employment of the Disabled (the word "Handicapped" is no longer politically correct) sent a lovely note remembering how you and I (with Loreen Arbus' help) started the Media Office and the whole ball rolling in our industry.

So many moons, so many changes.

And speaking of changes, the Soviet Union is no more. Gorby's out (but still alive, thank God), and Boris Yeltsin's in as president of Russia. Geographical boundaries have been drawn and redrawn. If my mother were alive today, how she would have laughed. Actually, that's not true—she would have cried to see so much waste, killing and destruction. And there would have been little cheer in seeing the realization of all her predictions about the economic woes that would beset us. So many of her forebodings have come true. Not because she was so brilliant, but because she had seen it all before.

The other day, by accident, a tape of an old David Wolper show came into my hands. It was a special from the early '80s about Nostradamus narrated by Orson Welles. Bob Guennette was one of the writers and directed it.

It's a fabulous show—and uncanny how many things Nostradamus predicted. It was also interesting to learn that one of the reasons he wrote so obscurely was to prevent repercussions to his family. I felt like there was a real reason the show had come into my hands, but I'm just not sure what it is. Unless it's to tell me not to plan on settling in Paris or New York—two prime targets according to Nostradamus, if World War III hasn't been averted by the new Russian/U.S. alliance.

$\sim\sim\sim$

I'm learning something from working on this book. I'm learning to change my work habits—to stifle the pencil-sharpening syndrome—not to "save the best for last."

Even as a child I would always leave the thing I liked best for last. When I ate (when we all still had meat every day), I would eat first the vegetables, then the potatoes and finally the meat. The trouble with that concept is, a lot of times you're too full, or it's too late, for the things you really wanted to have! (Although given our new dietary knowledge, especially the Pritikin credos, I was doing exactly the right thing!)

Now I've learned that if I want to work on this book—and I do because it brings me closer to you—I can't do everything else first. Because by the time I've finished paying the bills and writing letters and washing the dishes and making phone calls, it's too late and I'm too tired. So, now, I sit down to write this first.

And that's not hard to do because my head, and my heart, are clamoring to be with you, my love. This book is you—it's a testament to you, to our life together, and it gives me a chance to relive those precious moments. Thank you for all the love, for the happiness and for the years we had.

Paris, July 23, 1992

Norman, my love,

It's my last night in Paris. And what a beautiful night it is! The sky is like velvet—turning from a pale hue to royal to a dark midnight blue you can almost run your fingers through. It makes such a magnificent backdrop for the golden-lit monuments that are framed against the sky.

I took a break from packing around 9 p.m. to go watch the sunset. Right—9 p.m. is when the horizon starts to turn red. Remember Calgary—where sunset was at 10:30 p.m.—and how beautiful it was from the terrace of our penthouse apartment when we were there producing *Mr. Wizard's World*?

How sorry I am we never had a chance to visit the "Land of the Midnight Sun." My mother said it was magnificent. Or Australia (we were supposed to go to the Great Barrier Reef last year, remember?) Or the million other places I want to see with you—only you're not here to share them with me—and now it's painful to think of seeing all that beauty without you, and yet...

Tonight it was not so. This city that has been so nurturing, so spiritually healing, so helpful in easing the pain, came through right to the end.

I was packing and, for the first time since your death, I was not depressed. Not angry to be doing this alone—picking up stakes, moving again with all my things like a turtle with its house on its back.

I was organized, unpressured, relaxed—for once having given myself enough time to get everything done without having to pack until the crack of dawn.

As the setting sun cast its last, golden rays over the city, I threw on a pair of slacks and a jacket and left the apartment to walk "my neighborhood." And what a glorious neighborhood it is. The golden dome of the Invalides glistened and twinkled against the darkening sky. They regild it every 50 years. I was lucky they did it last year. It sparkled for me, like the precious jewel it is, every night.

At the corner I bought a popsicle, which I relished as the final treat before my serious dieting. (I've been going to the gym every day since mid-May and am determined to get my body back in shape. I'm even beginning to see some bones!)

As I crossed the Place d'École Militaire, I gazed up at the tip of the Eiffel Tower as it glistened through the leaves of the trees that were in full bloom this balmy night in late July. When I arrived last Autumn, the trees had already shed their leaves and the Tower was clearly visible from almost every corner of the square. Now, it peeked through the mantle of leaves and I had to walk to the very end of my terrace to get a good view of the Tower without the trees.

I arrived at the base of the Champ de Mars—the park that spreads its carpet leading up to the majestic Tower—and gazed around at all the splendor. It is incredible that it has remained unchanged for so many years. The Trocadero spreads its arms behind the Tower from the right bank, and no modern buildings have sprung up to spoil the view. The Eiffel Tower glistens as it was meant to—incredibly beautiful and alone, as it stretches its neck up towards the sky.

I sat down on the steps of a statue that salutes in the direction of the Tower. (I can't remember—or perhaps never knew—who it is. Some military man, I think, on horseback. You, of course, would have read every inscription and remembered it all!) I ate my ice cream and gazed at the beauty surrounding me—and I was at peace!

That seemed so incredible to me. Why wasn't I hurting? Why wasn't I sad to be leaving all this loveliness? This place where I felt I belonged? This place that helped me heal? And I somehow knew it was because I was heading somewhere else. Because this was the way it was meant to be. And I felt, somehow, I was also "heading home to you." Because I know that in Toronto I will have the time—and the inclination—to finish this book. I will be able to devote myself to it without the distractions.

Paris is a very seductive city. It steals your time, not because you necessarily do a lot of things—even though they are there for you to do. It steals your time because on every corner, on every street, there is a vista that sets you dreaming, that takes your mind back into the past. That makes you wonder about the people who designed the magnificent avenues and bridges and buildings. And the people who walked over them. So much to look at, so much to learn about, so much to turn your thoughts to.

Toronto won't be like that. There will be time—time to spend with you, talk to you, share with you, reach out to you. I know I must do that before I can move along my road—wherever it may lead.

You used to kid me that the way I went about my writing assignments was to start by cleaning the closets and handling everything I hadn't handled in the last 20 years. Then, when everything was absolutely, totally in order, I'd turn my attention to what I really had to do. (Which is why I wrote all my college papers during commercial breaks in the "Late, Late Show" the night before they were due!) You always teased me and called it my "pencil-sharpening" syndrome.

Well, the other day, for the first time, I suddenly realized if I continue to do what I've always done, I'll never get to finishing this book. And my whole life will change or—worse—stay the way it is.

So instead of paying the bills, writing the letters, getting everything out of the way and building up to what I really wanted to do, I simply reversed the process. And the words just poured out of me and before I knew it (only it was really several hours later), I had another 20 pages and a lot of thoughts—and had shed a lot of tears that had been building inside of me and had to get out. And I never got to the bills or the letters that weekend. But I had spent the day with you, healing in the process.

It had been a rainy Sunday, and as I walked home through the empty streets after the gym, the tears streamed down my cheeks and mingled with the rain on my face, and I thought about the lyrics from the Domenico Modugno song of years ago, "E piove, piove, sul nostro amore." Unfortunately, it will always be raining on our love from now on. The sun will never shine again on you and me.

But tonight, as I sat in the darkening twilight on my final evening in Paris, I finished my ice cream, gazed at the Eiffel Tower, smiled at the tourists with their children, taking pictures and playing ball, and didn't feel alone. I lit a cigarette and watched the night grow darker as the illuminated elevators made their way like fireflies up the girders of the Tower, past the Jules Verne restaurant on the second level, to the observation deck somewhere high in the sky.

And I looked over at a young woman who had been sitting on the stoop before I got there. And now there was a young man sitting next to her, smiling, trying to start a conversation, trying to pick her up. I remembered when those kinds of things used to happen to me. And I thought again of what Gloria had been saying to me about there being a message, vibrations, an odor if you will, that a woman sends out when she's available, when she's receptive, when she's looking. I tried to remember what that was like and when it had stopped happening to me.

It's not the first time I tried to remember when I had changed. When some things stopped being important. When they no longer mattered.

Some women never change. Like I told you, my aunt Yara flirted and cared about men as much when she was 80 as when she was 18. And men knew it and responded to it! Like the Gabor women and Liz Taylor and Marlene Dietrich and Sophia Loren—their image and perception of themselves never wavered. They love beautiful clothes, beautiful jewels and, above all, being women and loving men.

Yara would look at an attractive male, no matter what his age, and exclaim, "Now there's an interesting man!" And how she loved clothes! She would often extol how good a dress looked on her—even when she was 78! I would listen to her and watch her and wonder when did I stop being that way?

I read a lot as a teenager and went from Nancy Drew to psychology to philosophy. But it was Julie who introduced me to James Joyce with *Portrait of the Artist as a Young Man* and encouraged me to read David Reisman's *The Lonely Crowd* and later his *Faces in the Crowd*, but I still cared about hair, makeup, jewels and clothes back then.

So, I think it was Aldo, the irresistible Italian millionaire playboy-philosopher, who was hell-bent on self-destruction when I met him and who played women like a violin, who first made me see how empty I might have been.

And as far as men were concerned, I was on the road to great sexual fulfillment with my high school steady, Sy, but I loved Julie and then married Stan—so you can see how messed up things got to be.

Later, I guess I was too busy struggling for emotional and physical survival, and getting in and out of bad relationships, between the repressive '50s and the sexual revolution of the '70s, to focus much on the opposite sex.

And once there was you, there was no room for anyone else. No one was as loving, as caring, as gorgeous as you.

So, who remembers what it's really like to flirt? To send out the message that you're available? And where is that someone you want to send the message to? I guess that's really the key. It's not that I don't remember. I remember well what it's like to lock eyes with a handsome stranger across a crowded room, and have a whole conversation without saying a word, and have him follow you out of a restaurant because the attraction is too strong to deny. But where are those strangers today?

And who wants to risk being rejected? Not me—who always got what she wanted, when she wanted it.

I remember when I was 17. We were staying with a friend of my mother's in Rome and they were having a conversation about tantrums and my mother said, "Fern never has tantrums." Her friend replied, "Of course she never has tantrums. She doesn't have to—she always gets her way!" I thought she was crazy—just like I used to think people were crazy who used to tell me how strong I was. But now I realize she was right.

And that reminded me how, whenever I used to call out to you from another room, "Normy!," you would respond with, "What do you want?" And I would always answer you, "Got what I want!" So you had a sign made up that said that, and had it framed. It's still hanging at home on my office wall.

It was dark by the time I got up from the step, inhaled on my cigarette and said good-bye to the Eiffel Tower and Paris. As I started to inhale again, I was keenly aware that my throat felt raw and raspy, and the phlegm was building up at an alarming rate. I knew you were looking down and saying, "What are you doing—and why?"

And I remembered what Cory, my lovely ex-step-daughter, had said during her recent visit en route home from a sanatorium in Switzerland where she was recovering from a bout with a rare form of cancer: "It's not dying—we all have to die. It's the quality of life—or the quality of the dying—that you should think about."

And I know that cancer of the throat or lungs or vocal chords like my Uncle Dave had is an awful way to go. So, I went to throw out my cigarette, and this little voice inside me said, "Not just that one, all of them."

I hesitated because smoking had been a helpful crutch during these stress-filled months. But finally, I discarded my cigarette and stepped on the butt to extinguish the flame. Then I reached into my pocket, pulled out the pack and started to throw it away—but my frugality got the better of me. I put it carefully on a nearby ledge hoping some homeless cigarette addict might find it and be pleased.

And then I said a last good-bye to my Parisian neighborhood, and headed home, alone—and okay.

I've got to finish packing now. There's so much stuff, I have to leave three suitcases at Jean-Pierre's until I come back in September to pick them up. I know I'm coming back because Carla, Carlo and Titti's daughter, is getting married on the 13th and I'm going to Rome for her wedding. Stan and Joyce Black are supposed to be there, too. Remember that first night we introduced them, only a couple of summers ago?

When I talked to Ellen yesterday, I complained about how much stuff I had to pack. She said she wasn't surprised. After all, your pictures alone must fill an entire suitcase, she said! I laughed so hard—because she's right.

So, my darling, we're on our way again. I know we're heading down a new path, and it won't always be a smooth one. There will be challenges and hurdles. So stay close to me, and comfort me. Come—give me your hand.

Your loving wife,

Jern

Part II

*"We cannot discover new oceans
unless we have the courage to
lose sight of the shore."*
André Gide

Toronto, July 27, 1992

Normy,

I'm back at the Cambridge Suites (the same hotel I came to only 30 days after your death). I've just finished putting up your pictures, trying to make it feel more like home, even though I'll be traveling back and forth from here to New York, L.A. and Europe for the next—I don't know how many weeks...

And I remember last year's pain. That was one of those times when I thought I would be okay—it was a new hotel, we'd never been here. It was in a different neighborhood, not one that we had walked together. But when I checked in, I realized I was alone, so I holed up and went into denial.

The suite was like a cocoon, a womb where I could pretend you were someplace else—waiting for me, coming to me. So last spring, they had to pry me out of here with a crowbar. I kept telling our production coordinator I would move, take the apartment she had shown me—but next week. Or maybe next month. I kept putting it off.

I was so afraid. I knew subconsciously that moving into a real apartment would force me to face the fact that you weren't there.

Finally, everybody realized that I wasn't going to move without a push, so they said, "Fern, you're moving!" And I did and was eventually happier for it.

This year it's different. Things are beginning to change.

This year I can't wait to get into the apartment. (The same one I had last year is available and it's really great—with a 180-degree view of the city and the lake.) I'm even planning to entertain. And for the first time, the other day, when I thought of redecorating at least the loft back in our Marina del Rey home, it didn't trigger the Pavlovian response and sinking feeling in the pit of my stomach: "What? Move Normy's desk?! Disturb the pictures he hung on the wall? Turn 'his' office into mine? Impossible—I can't do it!"

It used to be, wherever I was, the thought of changing anything anywhere that was a part of "our life" would bring instant panic, dread and despair. So I guess it's getting better. Well, maybe not "better," but "easier" day by day.

As I unpacked, I ran across a sad reminder of last year. It's a letter I sent out to all our friends. One of the toughest, most painful, things to deal with after a death is telling the people who don't know. The ones who ask how you are and then are devastated to hear about your death because they simply didn't know—they hadn't heard—and they're afraid you may think they didn't care.

So, I sent this message as a way to tell people who didn't know—and to thank those that did for "being there."

CAMBRIDGE
·SUITES·
HOTEL

March 7, 1991

Dearest Friends:

It is with a very heavy heart that I write this letter.

As many of you already know, on January 3rd Norman, my
wonderful husband, lover, partner, best friend passed away
quickly, in his sleep. In less than an hour my life was
irrevocably changed - and a large void was created for all
of us.

However, your love, support, friendship, notes, letters,
donations and shared memories have underscored for me how
very special you all are - and how very special Norman was -
and continues to be - in all our hearts. Each and every one
of you will hear from me personally - but since I have
started work again - and am out-of-town, I wanted to get in
touch quickly, and to let you know I'm okay, and taking it
one day at a time. Some days are better than others - but
even in the tough moments - there will be a call, a note, an
invitation - one of you reaching out to ease the pain. I
want you to know it works and I appreciate your
thoughtfulness. You have brought me great comfort, and I am
so lucky to have you.

Currently I'm in Toronto, prepping another season of the USA
NETWORK series "COUNTERSTRIKE". My office number is: (416)
259-7684, and, as you can see, we are staying at the new
Cambridge Suites Hotel. Also, I can always be reached
through Brookfield Productions (213 390-9767), or our new
mailing address: 2554 Lincoln Blvd, #1079, Marina del Rey,
Ca. 90291. Please note that the Washington Place address is
no longer valid - and because I expect to be on location for
an extended period - I am not receiving mail at the home
address, either.

I love you. I thank you. And, I look forward to being in
touch with you soon.

Love,

Jerri

P.S. Many of you who were at the funeral have asked for a
copy of Mark's remarks. If you haven't received it yet -
please let me know and I'll get another out to you.

15 Richmond Street East
Toronto, Ontario M5C 1N2
Tel: (416) 368-1990 Fax: (416) 601-3751
Toll Free: 1-800-463-1990
LRI: 1-800-223-0888

I'm afraid I never got around to sending out Mark's eulogy as I had promised in that letter—but I have included it in here for everyone to read.

Why is the whole world suddenly only "thirtysome-thing"?

On a plane not long ago, a nice, attractive man sat next to me, and we were having a very pleasant conversation. I thought, "This is nice—I'm enjoying it. I wouldn't mind having dinner with him." Then he started telling me about a friend, and in the course of the story, he mentioned his friend was about "his age." And it turned out the friend was 39! Everybody I work with and know seems to be either 39 or 40. Isn't there anyone over 50 around (and available) these days?

I was talking to a cab driver yesterday. I have this fix-ation that I'm going to wind up with a taxi-cab driver somehow, someplace, because they seem to be the only men I talk to and get to know these days (except for my co-workers, who I just told you are all "underage"). I never have an opportunity to meet or talk to other men in other fields, but both here and in Paris I've met some really nifty cab drivers. (Of course, they were all mar-ried, too, but *c'est la vie*.)

Anyway, the driver was from Greece. He told me he couldn't wait to take his wife and go back there. As soon as his son gets married in a couple of months, they're off. He went on to say how much better he felt there because of the way people in Greece live their lives, and the warm, dry climate. Whenever he visits, within a few weeks, all his aches and pains disappear. He said people in his home town, not far from Athens, who are 60, all run around looking and feeling half their age. I told a few people that story and said I'm leaving for Greece on the next plane.

≈ ∼ ≈

I called Aldo in Italy to say good-bye before I left Paris and learned that Jerry had passed away.

How kind God was to let me see him—in good shape—before he died. What a gift that was, and what a gift the things he told me. I can only imagine how much Aldo and Letizia will miss him. Aldo has probably lost his one remaining true—and closest—friend.

I remember that day last fall up in the mountains when I walked into Aldo's restaurant and at first saw this stranger, this elderly man. The man smiled and I recognized Jerry, as the years washed away. And on the way home, as he drove Branka and me back to Rome—after he finished telling me how crazy Aldo had been about me—he turned his attention to the present, pulled out his gun and offered me his services! In case I needed anything taken care of! And I've just run across a note he sent me in November of last year, giving me the phone number of a friend in Paris I never got around to calling. He said he would be seeing "Squacci" (his nickname for Aldo) in the next few days, and offered, "Should you need me for whatever." He was 75 years old if he was a day, and he was offering me his services as a "hit man" for Heaven's sake!

Aldo told me how painful it was for him the last time he went to see Jerry in the hospital. Jerry didn't recognize him, was totally out of it and bore no resemblance to his former self. Aldo said he regretted having gone to the hospital because he would have preferred to remember Jerry as he had been.

I understood so well what he was saying. It was one of the reasons I had not gone into the emergency room when they told me you were dead. But now, how very much I wish I had!

I wish I had held you in my arms and blessed you on your way, and that I had not been afraid to see any pain you might have felt. I just could never bear the thought that you had suffered in any way. But how I wish now that I had followed your stretcher into the emergency room, pushed my way in.

I wish I had been with you, my darling love. You should not have had to die with strangers.

Normy,

Well, my darling, it's been an eventful two weeks! On the 7th I had to fly down to New York for a PR meeting on the show, and to attend Michael's and Gloria's birthday party in West Hampton on the weekend. It was his 65th! I won't give away her age—but she's younger than me. In fact, last year she sent me a great birthday card. On the front it said, "Happiness is being able to wish your best friend Happy Birthday." And on the inside it said, "Ecstasy is knowing you're younger than she is!"

So Friday morning I got to the airport only to discover that I had left my passport in the hotel suite! There was no way I could get back and forth in time to retrieve it. Nor would there be time for my secretary, Keitha, to go to the hotel and bring it to me.

I checked with the airline, but there were no later flights I could take and still make the meeting. The airline attendant asked if I didn't have some other document or identification. I said, "Sure, driver's license, credit cards, etc." "The drivers license will do," she assured me, so I thought, "I'll try it—what the heck."

I got to the U.S. Immigration counter and gave the officer my story as I gingerly pushed my California driver's license in his direction, telling him the airline assured me it would suffice.

He picked up the license with great disdain, examined it, then barely looked at me and said, "So what does this tell me? Only that you can drive a car in California!" I was really miffed.

I explained again how I had left my passport at the hotel, but he really didn't care. Then suddenly he asked where I was born. My brain went into overdrive and processed quicker than a computer chip. I realized instantly that if I said, "Italy," I was finished. They'd probably haul me away. So I quickly whispered, "L.A.," as if whispering would somehow make it okay to lie. He countered just as quickly, "What's the capital of California?"

I was speechless. That really caught me off guard and my mind went blank. "What?" I asked, shaking my head to clear the cobwebs away. "What's the capital of California?" he repeated. And while the word "Fresno" kept swirling through my head, I blurted, "Sacramento" and he let me go on my way!

(When I told that story at Michael and Gloria's party, someone said I should have answered, "So, what's that going to tell you? Only that I know geography!")

It's surprising the places in which I most feel the grief. In California, and other places where I have to drive, it's the car.

I remember Bonnie Hammer asked me shortly after you passed away how I was getting on. And I told her it was funny, but it really got to me when I was driving by myself. And she told me after her father died, she, too, would find tears streaming down her cheeks when she was alone in her car. And I suddenly realized that those first months when I got to Toronto after the funeral, I subconsciously resisted getting my own vehicle. I would have Keitha pick me up and drive me home. Some unconscious mechanism was protecting me from a situation I somehow knew would be too hard to take.

Of course, when I went home for a few days, there would be no alternative. L.A. is not a place where you can avoid driving by yourself. My sensations alternated from deep mourning to that strange, unreal feeling I first experienced right after the funeral. The feeling that a whole chunk of my life had just disappeared, gone away, was negated, as if it had never been.

But when a particular song that recalled our past, like "If It Takes Forever, I Will Wait For You" from *The Umbrellas of Cherbourg*—or one that echoed my present thoughts like Bette Midler's rendition of "Wind Beneath My Wings"—the tears would flow and my sense of loss was monumental.

Finally, I learned to use those times to get some of the crying out of my system. Tears I had held in, tears I had denied. And driving my own car became okay.

In fact, it became so okay that one glorious Saturday last summer I had an irresistible urge to go for a very fast ride in a sportscar with the top down, wind blowing through my hair. Kind of like the way I used to do in Rome on the Raccordo Annulare when I would push the first sportscar I ever owned to 150 km. per hour when I was young and carefree.

I checked the yellow pages and learned that unlike LALA land, Toronto has no rental companies that have wild and wonderful cars just for the asking. So, on Monday I talked to our transportation captain and he said he'd see what he could do.

What he could do turned out to be a great little black Porsche Carrera, and when I rented it, the news traveled through the two production companies on our lot like wildfire. I said had I known it was going to cause such a stir and have everyone talking about me, I would have done it sooner.

I guess it was funny. The middle-aged lady supervising producer of the show tooling around in a jazzy Carrera, while the sexy star drove around in a standard four-door sedan. (This season Simon has a Porsche and I'm going to bring up our stuffy four-door Cadillac DeVille.)

But right now, for a couple of weeks, I have the Carrera again. And what I love most about it is the "hug" you get from the seat. It kind of cradles your body and every morning makes me feel snug and cozy. It's as if the car is saying, "I'm so glad you're here!" But the other night that car almost got me into a heap of trouble, and hearing about it would have made you a nervous wreck.

I was working late at the office on a story for *Counterstrike* that I titled, "The Midnight Caller." It's about a stalker, and I was scaring myself to death.

As you may remember, our offices are on the beautiful but deserted grounds of an abandoned psychiatric hospital in the Western suburbs of Toronto. The security guard always walks us to our cars when we leave after dark. It was close to midnight when Keitha and I called it a wrap and Mick and his dog Brandy walked us to our cars. I got into the Porsche, still a little spooked from the story, and looked at the mysterious moon peaking through the clouds and reflecting on the branches of the nearby trees and realized that I didn't remember how to lock the doors of the car from the inside anymore.

But, so what? I started the motor and drove off the grounds and onto the Expressway. A few blocks before I got to the hotel, while stopped at a red light, I glanced into my rear view mirror. There was a car right behind me with a man at the wheel—and I got this very strange feeling. Of course, I rationalized the situation: It is the downtown area of a busy city. To have a car behind you at a stop light is not an unnatural thing.

I headed toward the hotel and he followed. Okay. It is, after all, a hotel, I told myself. You are not the only guest they have.

I pulled into the driveway, as did he. I headed down the garage ramp, and he was right behind me.

As always, I try to get as close to the elevator access as possible, because I'm usually carrying at least 50 pounds of scripts, a computer, etc. So, I continued on down to the second level. As I did, I talked to myself. "Okay, there are a lot of parking spots on level one so if he comes down to level two, there is definitely something strange."

I pulled into a spot by the wall. He appeared in my rear view mirror and pulled into a space not far from me.

Now, I had heard voices and noticed some people right by the door leading to the elevator lobby, unloading their car as I pulled in. The man following me got out of his car and disappeared through the doorway as I assessed the situation. There was no way I could get all my things and make it to the elevator in time to go up with the other people. So, I decided the alternative was to stall for time, hoping he would go up with the other people, leaving the coast clear for me.

I dallied as long as I could and then, laden with totes and scripts, I finally locked my car and walked slowly toward the elevator lobby.

The garage was lit like high noon, so it was hard to get spooked or take my fear seriously. There were no shadows or hiding places. And he had looked like a perfectly ordinary man. Beige slacks and short-sleeved shirt, nondescript hair, altogether unimpressive.

As I walked, my conversation with myself continued. "Now, if he's waiting in the vestibule, there is definitely something wrong." Luckily, as I got closer to the door, I glimpsed an arm and an elbow through the glass panel. He was waiting for me.

I stopped, turned slowly and headed back toward my car—still talking to myself. "You're being silly," this little voice said. "He looked perfectly harmless. You're only two stories down from the street level—there's a whole city up there. People. Life. What could happen in that short distance, that short expanse of time that it would take to get from here to there?"

Fortunately this other voice said, "What could happen? He could have a gun! He could have a knife!"

"Okay, okay," I replied and got into the car and started the motor. As I began to drive away, in my rear view mirror I saw the man look out through the glass panel in the door to see what I was doing and what was taking me so long!

I drove up to the street level and heaved a great sigh of relief. What could have happened? I don't know. Perhaps a robbery at best. A rape or murder at worst. Who knows what passed through that man's head—except that he saw a woman alone, late at night, driving an expensive car.

How sad that times have changed so much—all over the world—since I used to drive alone to watch the sunrises in Rome. And in New York, late at night, I used to walk the city streets!

I remember when we were in Italy together in '88 having dinner on the beautiful patio of Michele and Marta's home in Tivoli overlooking the valley that leads to Rome. Michele told the story about sleeping in the unfinished house when they came back from their honeymoon in the '60s—without windows and doors. And now, they've been burglarized over and over again and they sleep behind locked doors and bolted windows! Why have we all decided to accept this as a way things have to be?!

In the brief span of time since you're not here, evolution has taken on a strange, new meaning. Anti-theft systems have improved so much on cars that thieves are now resorting to "carjacking" (a new word has entered the language). They simply get you at a light or in a parking lot, pull a gun and insist on getting the keys. The Auto Club has even come out with a set of "Safety Steps for Motorists." Among other things, they advise you to be aware of your surroundings at all times; to use the middle lane when traveling in risky neighborhoods; to leave enough room between you and the next car so you can pull away at a light if you have to; to be suspicious of minor rear-end accidents; to know the area you're going to be driving through; and to always have enough gas. I remember how many times you would let the gauge go right to empty!

More and more people are afraid to leave their homes—even in daylight! Lois got mugged in New York at high noon on East 36th Street! She lost her bag and a number of teeth!

In the '60s, our musings about changes were on a lighter note. Times seemed so much simpler then. I ran across this ditty among my souvenirs at home from the days when I used to do translations. It's titled "Remember" and appeared in the Fun & Games column of the *ATA (American Translators Association) Newsletter.*

> *Remember when hippie meant big in the hips?*
> *And trip involved travel in cars, planes and ships?*
> *When pot was a vessel for cooking things in*
> *And hooked was what Grandmother's rug might*
>   *have been?*
> *When fix was a verb that meant mend or repair,*
> *And be-in meant well-organized, tidy and clean,*
> *And grass was a ground cover, normally green?*
> *When groovy meant furrowed with channels and*
>   *hollows*
> *And birds were winged creatures, like robins and*
>   *swallows?*
> *When fuzz was a substance, real fluffy, like lint,*
> *And bread came from bakeries—not from the mint.*
> *When roll meant a bun, and rock was a stone*
> *And hang up was something you did with the phone?*
> *It's groovy, Man, groovy, but English it's not*
> *Methinks that our language is going to pot.*

Of course, my favorite poem from that era used to be on napkins at the Monkey Bar of the Hotel Élysées. (I saw my friend Leon Quain, the owner, on one of my recent trips to New York. He hasn't changed a bit, but they don't have those napkins in the bar anymore.)

I was meeting Brooks Arthur there to discuss his producing the English-language recording of *The Mysterious Voyage of Marie-Rose*. The poem went like this:

Three monkeys sat in a coconut tree,
Discussing things as they're said to be.
Said one to the others, "Now listen, you two,
There's a certain rumor that can't be true—
That man descended from our noble race—
The very idea is a disgrace!
No monkey ever deserted his wife,
Starved her babies and ruined her life.
And you've never known a mother monk
To leave her babies with others to bunk.
Or to pass them on from one to another
'Til they scarcely know who is their mother.
And another thing you'll never see—
A monk build a fence 'round a coconut tree,
And let the coconuts go to waste,
Forbidding all other monks a taste.
Why if I put a fence 'round a coconut tree,
Starvation would force you to steal from me.
Here's another thing a monk won't do—
Go out at night and get on a stew,
Or use a gun or club or knife
To take some other monkey's life.
Yes, man descended—the ornery cuss—
But, brother, he didn't descend from us!"

In transit, en route to L.A., August 30, 1992

Norman, my love,

So often, in the years before you, when I was very unhappy, unspeakably sad, with the hurt welling up inside and nowhere to go, I would describe the feeling as a "stomach full of tears." Now, after you, when the realization overcomes me—and I plunge into the sadness and despair, the unbearable sense of loss—I call the feeling a "heart" full of tears.

You are gone forever. I'm sitting on a plane heading home to L.A., and there's an empty seat beside me. And an empty home waiting for me and I can't hold back the tears. The summer's almost over and Joey's bat mitzvah is next week. (Yes, your beautiful niece is almost 13 years old!)

My horoscopes this spring (the ones from magazines—not anything done especially for me) kept saying I would find love and romance this summer. That hasn't happened—or maybe, in a way, it did. This year, as I reviewed and relived our life together, thanks to this book, I fell in love with you all over again.

So many things trigger memories of you and of our relationship. I see a colleague going through a mid-life crisis and I remember the one you were in when we met. How unhappy we both were—and how desperately we needed what the other had to give!

I remember the guilt, too. Yours and mine, when we contemplated what pain our happiness might bring to others. Me, in so much emotional turmoil that I longed for the sanctuary of a padded cell, married to a spouse who threatened suicide every time I suggested we separate.

And you—you were going through so much soul-searching, seeing your business falling apart, perhaps going down the drain, feeling people only looked to you to pay the bills, and wondering what it was all about anyway. Your anguish was so palpable, so raw, I tried to put your thoughts into words (and a lot of my feelings were there, too), in a poem I hoped would help you make whatever choice you had to make:

Gone Fishin'

Just say that I've gone fishin'—
*   or—"off to see the world."*
Tell my friends I'll miss them—
*   tell my folks I'll call.*
This is better than a letter
*   'cause what all could I say—*
That would explain to those who love me
*   just why I went away?*
There's more to life than breathin',
*   There's more to me than clay,*
There's more to taste than eatin',
*   And so I've gone away.*
I'm off to seek my maker—
*   I'm off to find out life—*
And when she comes, I'll take 'er—
*   the good—and all the strife.*
I'm not runnin' like a coward,
*   I'll walk with head held high,*

Letters to My Husband

I'm off to seek my maker,
*   I'm off to reach the sky.*
It's not that I don't love you all—
*   that you're not good to me—*
It's just that time is passin'
*   and I've been cheatin' me.*
There's more to life than workin'—
*   There's more to me than that.*
There's more to love than screwin'
*   And just lyin' on one's back.*
I'm off to climb that mountain,
*   I'm off to touch the sky,*
'Cause when I lie there dyin',
*   I'm gonna want to know just why.*
I'm gonna want to say: "I've been there!
*   I've been to hell and back!*
And then I climbed that mountain,
*   though my world seemed out of whack.*
I did it, God, I did it.
I struggled and I cried,
But I've lived a life worth livin',
I did not live a lie.
I felt with all my being,
I gave with all my might,
The price was not a small one,
The pain reached every height.
But it took me on my journey,
And has brought me to your gate,
And now as I lie dyin',
I can smile, at peace, and wait.

> *'Cause I have lived a life worth livin',*
> *I have laughed and I have cried,*
> *I have loved with all my bein',*
> *Now I can bid this world good-bye."*
> *Yes—when I meet my maker—*
> *When the end is clear in sight—*
> *Let me know my life's a true one—*
> *Let my heart be proud and light.*
> *So, just say that I've gone fishin'—*
> *that I'm "off to see the world."*
> *Yes, tell them I've gone fishin'—*
> *fishin' for my life.*

You could substitute the words "kids" and "wife" for "friends" and "folks," but we were still in the closet, not an "item" yet.

It's interesting to read those words after all these years and to know that you made your choice and that it was the right one for you, and certainly the one I made was right for me. We did laugh and cry and suffer and make a difference, and because you told me so often, I know that you did love me "with all your being" (as I loved you) and that your heart was "proud and light."

Your friend, Bea Meshekow, told me after the memorial service last year—when I read my first letter to you—that my love for you is incredible. That I've put you on a pedestal and created someone who didn't exist. She wasn't being mean-spirited, she was just expressing a thought. I wondered a lot about that, especially because I, and all your friends, remember a very different man than your children, at least your daughters, remember you to be.

It's funny: They are jealous of the affection and love you gave to me—and even to your friends—because they think they never got that. Remember how I used to complain that you had always "taken care of" Anita and the kids and you had never financially taken care of me? What's that saying about the grass always being greener...?

I couldn't get into it with them, because so much of how children perceive their parents comes out of the relationship between the mother and the father—and how each parent portrays the other to the kids. But I think your children felt abandoned every time you went away on a business trip. And since sales took you on the road from Monday to Friday every week when they were little, they couldn't understand your coming back and wanting to pick up where things had been.

Anyway, when I had a chance, I asked Bea what she had meant. She told me I was creating someone who was perfect—and you were far from that. "After all," she said, "Norman had a wife and children when he met you..." And yet, you started seeing me.

The "creating someone perfect" really got to me because I know part of what you learn in "mourning" groups or counseling is that the departed partner was not perfect—and we mustn't make them that—or we will never find anyone to fill the bill.

But I don't think that's what I'm doing. And I'm not making up the hundreds of letters and phone calls about you that I have received. I know you weren't perfect and, God knows, neither am I. But when you look at the total picture, we cared about each other. In the middle of all the pain—or the anger—we cared not about ourselves, we cared about the "other." We were friends first and lovers second. Your pain was my pain, and when you listened to my troubles, you truly heard what I was saying. Just as my first husband had ignored me and my second try at marriage made me nuts—you made me whole. You healed me.

I used to say that we all go through life with "baggage," the sum total of all our problems, neuroses, etc. Some of us are lucky and we never have to open the suitcases. But once we do, we can't go on with our lives until we've taken care of the garbage. It was my relationship with Konny that opened my "suitcases" and forced me to face all my "garbage." It was my relationship with you that got rid of it. And I know I was there to take away some of your pain.

I remember how when we first met we would talk into the small hours of the night—watching our "stock" (as you would call it) go up on the electronic Newsweek clock that we could see from most of your New York hotel room windows—3 and 4 a.m. were not unusual hours for us in those days.

We told each other the stories of our lives—things we hadn't shared with anyone—before we had any idea what our future lives might be. I remember early on when I would ask what I could do for you to take away your hurting, you would say, "Just be there." So I wrote:

Be There

Be there, as you were that night,
to share my fate with me,
When two paths cross the way ours did
it must be Destiny.
Be there, in my heart and soul
to share each day with me,
Be there, though our love's untold
except in reverie.
Be there now to hold my hand,
and when you're far away,
Be there when I close my eyes
to guide me on my way.
Be there always, soft yet strong
to hold me and caress me
Be there though you're far away
with tenderness possess me.
Be there to accept my love
the essence of my being
Be there—in any way you can—
to give my whole life meaning.

Thank you, my darling, for being there—even now.
For doing all those things for me, and for being the kind-
est, sweetest, gentlest man I ever met.

Normele,

So I went to Joey's bat mitzvah in L.A. She's such a lovely young lady now, I wish you could see her. In fact, all the children in the family are blossoming—and your granddaughter is incredible. A "little girl" carbon copy of her brother, who's now a gorgeous young man. I know you would just eat her up if you could see her.

Remember when you flew back from Toronto for Philip's 50th birthday? I was doing *Heartsounds* or *Kane & Abel*, or whatever, and didn't feel I could leave my job to accompany you. If I knew then what I know now, I would have flown back with you—cherished every moment of every year. But those were the days when I spent every waking minute on the set. I was "on the line," and lived, ate and breathed the job at hand.

I've changed. And it's not just that I'm running (which I know I am), it's that life is special, relationships are precious, people are important. Like my mother used to say, it's important to spend time with, do things for, the living. Better to go to weddings and bat mitzvahs than funerals and hospitals. As Robin's friend Joanie put it (yes, they both flew down from San Francisco and we were all together and thrilled), our family can be a lot of fun when we get together for happy occasions.

That's why I flew to Boston to meet Philip and Ellen for his birthday, invited the world to visit me in Paris and, on September 12, was in Rome for Carla Mariotti's wedding—a week after the bat mitzvah in L.A.! Life is short, so what the hell! Of course, it was beautiful. Carla looked absolutely lovely, and you know Carlo—he had fireworks and a marching band. By the end of the evening, the young people were throwing each other into the pool, designer clothes, Bulgari jewelry, and all!

And today, Rosh Hashana, I am in West Hampton with Michael and Gloria and their friends. I flew in yesterday, and Sonny Grosso happened to be on the same plane again. I "knew" that was going to happen because I had had my hair colored that morning!

Only this time the color was okay and, since I'd had a premonition that I should look presentable, I'd dressed and put on makeup. Sonny kidded me that he'd expected me to have colored my hair! You see I'd given him the first half of this manuscript, so he'd read about that infamous three-color escapade. And guess what? The man who gives notes on Shakespeare didn't have one note on this book! He loved it, said it "makes you laugh and makes you cry," and he thought it would make a great one-woman play. Some other people have said the same thing.

I had also sent Sonny a copy of the short story I had written based on what you told me about the day your father died. Sonny was also 12 when his father passed away, so I knew he would relate.

Even though the story was meant for your eyes only, I "changed the names to protect the innocent," made the grocery store a hardware store, called you "Michael" and your dad "David" and gave you a baby sister and younger twin siblings instead of Natalie and Philip.

In those days, I was always "protecting" and hiding, in case my writings should fall into the wrong hands and my love for you would shine between the lines.

Do you remember "Trolley Ride To Manhood"?

"Trolley Ride To Manhood"
by Fern Field

"Send Michael down to the store," her husband's voice was strained. "I'm coming home. He can help Irving."

"What's wrong, David? What happened?" Her fear was instantaneous and ill-concealed.

"Nothing happened. I don't feel well, that's all. I'm coming home."

"David, you're sick?" The tears were mirrored in her voice.

"Esther!" he said sharply, then more gently, wearily, "I'm all right. Don't worry. Send Michael. I'll see you soon."

David replaced the receiver slowly. He was too tired for his 37 years. He glanced from the storeroom into the hardware store. His brother Irving was putting merchandise on the newly installed shelves. The expansion, the redecorating had been a little too much, David thought to himself. A few hours rest would restore him.

He turned and took his jacket from the rack nearby. A sharp pain in his chest made him wince and he caught a glimpse of his ashen face in the mirror hanging haphazardly on the wall beside him.

Maybe it's indigestion, he thought as he walked out into the store.

Irving turned and frowned at the sight of his older brother.

"Irving, Michael will be here to help you close up. I'm going home now." Irving nodded and watched as David walked slowly out the door. He stood riveted to the spot until David had entered his car and driven off down the street.

~ ~ ~

Esther replaced the receiver and tried not to cry, but her panic was overwhelming. David was never sick. In their 14 years of marriage he had never missed a day at the store, never closed up early. He was a hard worker and provided well for her and their four children in these difficult times.

Now David was coming home. At three o'clock! And he had asked her to send Michael, their firstborn, to the store. Something was wrong and Esther was afraid. What would become of her? Of the children? If anything happened to David, how could they go on?

~ ~ ~

Michael looked out the trolley window and watched the houses go by. To ride alone to his father's store was a rare treat for him. Usually his mother said he was too young to go by himself. And on those occasions when he did go alone, she would walk him to the trolley stop and his father or his uncle would pick him up at the other end. But today was different.

Michael knew that the minute he had walked into the house. His baby sister was crying, the twins were fighting and his mother looked distraught and more frail than usual.

"Michael," she had said quietly, "go help Uncle Irving close up the store. Papa asked me to send you. He has to come home early."

Michael thought she would continue, but she had said nothing more. He had put his books on the table, taken the coins his mother held out for him and walked out the door into the cold, winter afternoon.

The usual elation at being allowed to go somewhere alone was missing today. Somehow he felt somber—grey—like the clouds in the sky.

Now, as he looked out the trolley window, it began to drizzle. Michael smiled as he thought how worried his mother would get at his walking in the rain, but then his smile faded. Today she would not be thinking of him. Somehow he knew this.

Suddenly, his father's battered old station wagon came into view.

"Hey, Dad!" Michael mouthed soundlessly, as he knocked on the window pane trying to get his father's attention.

"Dad," Michael waved and tried to open the window. But it was stuck.

Michael felt an irresistible urge to jump off the trolley and go to his father. But he had been told to go to the store and Michael was a good boy—an obedient one. And anyway, just as he was about to get off, the light changed and his father's car turned right and disappeared as the trolley proceeded on down the hill. Michael sat back and felt a strange sense of loss as the familiar landscape went by.

$\backsim \sim \backsim$

When Uncle Irving brought Michael home a few hours later, his father was already dead.

Michael reeled at the news, though he had somehow expected it. He looked around seeing everything for the first time, his eyes filled with unspoken and unrelieved pain.

His mother was sitting on the edge of the couch, her body racked by her silent, dry sobs. She had been crying, but there were no more tears now—only the grief.

She looked up as they came in and Michael was stunned by her youthfulness. She looks like a kid, Michael thought suddenly. Like my kid sister.

Michael sat down by his mother and she ran her fingers through his thick, dark hair. Tears welled up in her eyes at the sight of her 12-year-old son. Esther took Michael's hands.

"Michael, my son...my son," she sobbed. "You're the man in the family now," she said, condemning the boy to manhood.

Michael pulled back, stunned by her words. But his mother looked helpless, defenseless. He put his arm around her shoulders and held her tight.

"Don't worry, Momma," he comforted bravely. "I'm here now. It's okay. I'll take care of everything. I promise I will."

(Normy, I should have added the words: "And he did!")

Normele, my darling,

It's the beginning of another Jewish New Year. In 10 days I will be back in L.A. for Yom Kippur. I want to share that with you there—with the people who love you. I want to go to the cemetery, to be in our home for that most solemn day.

On the plane last Saturday, Sonny told me how touching he thought the story was about your father—especially the line, "Don't worry, Momma, I'm here now. It's okay. I'll take care of everything. I promise I will." He had had the same experience. He, too, was out when his father died and his mother and sisters all lit up when he walked in. They, too, looked upon him as their "strength and savior." Your story brought back a lot of bittersweet memories, he said. And he, like you, also thought he was going to die young, like his father had. I told him how you were convinced you were going to die at 37, and how you made out your will, got all your affairs in order and took that trip around the world with Anita when you were 35, because there weren't going to be many years left.

I remember your telling me how impressed you were at the time that you were able to take that trip. How you marveled at how far from your family's small grocery store in Chicago you had come. And you never lost that sense of wonder—you were always just like a little kid. Wherever we went, whatever we did, you always got the biggest kick.

And then Sonny started to pull out some mementos he carries with him. One was a poem his sister had written and as I looked at it my eyes immediately filled with tears. It reminded me of a little poem I had cut out of a magazine, when I was a just a little girl. It's pasted into my giant scrapbook that is now falling apart but filled with so many tidbits I saved up through the years. It's called "Grandmother's Message," by Jane Merchant. It goes like this:

> *"Give my love to Laura,*
> *Give my love to Jim."*
> *Wherever gramps was going,*
> *Gran sent her love by him.*
> *"Give my love to Susan,*
> *Give my love to Todd."*
> *Last night she whispered gently,*
> *"Give my love to God."*

Sonny's sister called her poem: "Lily & Ben Together Again," and it begins...

> *He stood just inside Heaven's gate*
> *looking so forlorn.*
> *He saw her smile, his face lit up,*
> *He asked, "What took so long?"*

Well, that really got to me. I could see you standing up there, waiting for me, and thinking what's taking her so long? And should it—will it—take "so long"? What am I doing down here that's so important? Is there really a reason for me to be here and you up there?

LILY & BEN
TOGETHER AGAIN

He stood just inside Heaven's gate
looking so forlorn.
He saw her smile, his face lit up,
He asked, "What took so long?"

Her eyes met his and
shone with love.
You knew she missed him too.
She whispered, as she took his hand,
"I had a lot to do.

When God chose to take you home,
Me he did not warn.
Only two years had gone by,
since our youngest child was born.

Our son, so devastated,
forced to take a grown man's role,
was not quite ready for
a family to control.

Two daughters. One so fragile,
with insecurities and fear.
The other, not much older,
Couldn't fathom life so severe.

Imprisoned by grief and love for them
I knew not where to start.
The one that rocked their cradle,
Now had a rope around her heart.

Where to start without you,
My man so firm and strong,
Always so protective
when anything went wrong.

I struggled for solutions,
even thought of suicide,
But with God's help the kids grew up
with love and inner-pride.

Sonny's success within the Law
beyond our fondest dreams,
Yet, felt the loss that you were not
there to share the scene.

As years went by our daughters blessed
with children of their own.
One sought, also, to nurse the sick,
the other hearth and home.

While fighting pressure from her peers,
and demons of the times,
Our youngest misconstrued my love
to be a trap that binds.

When illness struck
they helped me through
to conquer my despair.
Even though I longed for you,
I could not leave them there.

Until I felt my work was done
and they could carry on..."
"I know," he said, "I saw it all."
Then wrapped her in his arms.

"I can't answer," he explained,
"For decisions God has done,
but I was there to witness
each new milestone with our son.

I watched him stave off injuries
adversity and doubt.
In that fire, when engulfed in flames,
I helped the blind man guide him out.

The survivor sister had become
with a will so deep and strong;
In time enabled her twins
to make it on their own.

Though 'Peanuts' found it difficult
her feelings to express
The roles she chose, to nurse and write,
is how she did it best.

When you moved to rural grounds
and bought that modest home
I knew my "Tiger-Lil" resolved
to make it on her own.

Our young Celeste, missed the father
she never really knew.
The loneliness and grief she felt
sadly transferred to you.

Like an Angel on their shoulder
You let them spread their wings and fly.
Now they must shape the legacy
Begun by you and I.

So, do not be disheartened
for our daughters and our son.
God has sent you back to me.
We'll watch, together, 'til they come."

LGV 9/24/92

Sonny pulled out another item that, coincidentally, is almost exactly like one I found among your papers just the other day. It's about not trying to be so perfect.

If I Had My Life to Live Over Again
by Nadine Stair, 85 years old, Louisville, Kentucky

If I had to live my life over I'd dare to make more mistakes next time. I'd relax. I would limber up. I'd be sillier than I have been this trip. I would take fewer things seriously. I would take more chances. I would take more trips. I would climb more mountains, swim more rivers. I would eat more ice cream and less beans. I would perhaps have more actual troubles, but I'd have fewer imaginary ones.

You see I'm one of those people who live seriously and sanely hour after hour, day after day. Oh, I've had my moments, and if I had to do it over again, I'd have more of them. In fact, I'd try to have nothing else. Just moments, one after another, instead of living so many years ahead of each day. I've been one of those persons who never goes anywhere without a thermometer, a hot water bottle, a raincoat and a parachute. If I had to do it over again, I would travel lighter than I have.

If I had to live my life over, I would start barefoot earlier in the spring and stay that way later in the fall. I would go to more dances. I would ride more merry-go-rounds. I would pick more daisies.

Toronto, October 3, 1992

Norman, my sweetheart,

I thought here in Toronto, unlike Paris, I would stop and take stock, work on the book, think about my life. The truth is, since I arrived I've been running at top speed—hoping, I guess, that the reality wouldn't catch up with me. Today I stopped running for a minute and the pain caught up with me and gripped me in its vise.

It's scary for someone like me, who doesn't really like to show her emotions, how close to the surface the pain really is now.

Having decided I could not bury myself in *Counterstrike* any longer—and without the incredible beauty of Paris to distract me—I've made sure not to leave a moment free just to stop and think. Since I arrived here I've managed to travel almost every weekend—New York, West Hampton, L.A., Paris, Rome. It's taking its toll.

Last night I was having dinner with a friend, Vincent Fournier, one of our writers from Paris, and we were talking about how much traveling takes out of you. "But how come the jet-setters always look so good?" I asked. He said simply, "They don't have to work. They can rest when they get there." I guess he's right—and I wonder how many of them are running like me. I've managed to book myself straight through the New Year.

But I wasn't running today. Today is Saturday and I was alone—for the first time since I can't remember when. I had some errands I needed to do. I walked up Yonge Street and thought of you. I went into a wonderful store, the Novelty Shoe Company, where they rebuild old shoes. The owner is such a nice man—you would have loved him and you would have become instant friends. He's been there for 56 years! And he says he's still there because he's still having fun and, like you, he loves people. He told me about a couple from Israel who was in his store the other day and how he would have loved to have taken them home because they were so interesting, but they had a plane to catch. It reminded me of the owner of that tiny grocery store in New Zealand you made friends with, who was so devastated when you told him we were going home in a few days, because he had wanted to invite you to his home.

As I paid for my shoe and bag repair, he admired the quality of the handbag and I mentioned I'd bought it many years ago in Rome. "How I would love to have the time to talk to you," he said to me. "I haven't had the opportunity to travel much and I love to hear about all the places people have been." As I walked out, I contemplated how many things we take for granted, all the places we've been to, the things we've done and seen, and I thought how sorry I am he never met you. He would have loved you—and you would have made a new friend.

Then I walked to Tea Masters and sat looking out at the small park that's across from 30 Wellington Street, the building we lived in during *Heartsounds* and *Kane & Abel*. I knew I didn't want a world without you in it, and I wondered if I could just go back in time, perhaps you would still be here. When I think that I can't reach you, call you, hold you, the pain is really too great to bear. No wonder I keep running and surrounding myself with people and things to do. The alternative is too hard and devastating. And yet as I walked the streets today, I kept telling myself, "You have to feel the pain. You can't keep pushing it away, burying it, denying it." But to think about it and accept it, means to drown in such deep despair that I can't do it.

I understand now why in times gone by, the bereaved used to tear their clothes and rant and rave. The pain needs to be heard. But today, we're all so prim and proper. I mean, I would never let the world see me that way. Writing this is the closest I can get to showing the hurt, and some people will think this is too private, too intimate to share. But for me, it's too painful to contain.

I remember the weekend after your funeral, our grandson Adam came to spend the night with me. He was only 9 and had already had his share of pain—first his great grandmother, then his grandmother and now you. We made plans to go to a movie and decided *Kindergarten Cop* would be the thing. Then, as we approached the theater in Century City, Adam asked if we could go see *Home Alone* instead. "But you've seen it three times already," I protested. "I know," he nodded, "but let's go anyway."

That night when his mother called and asked what we did, I heard him tell her we'd seen *Home Alone* again. She must have asked why on earth we did that, because I heard him explaining, and I was stunned to hear him answer with a wisdom far beyond his years, "We really needed to laugh today."

By the way, I told him you had taken me to see it—even though you'd gone with him the first time he saw it. He asked if we'd both laughed. I said, "A lot," and then we both giggled as he told me how embarrassed he was because you had laughed so hard in the theater with him. I'm sitting here grinning now because I can just see your beautiful face all crinkly, and laughing so hard the tears are streaming down your cheeks!

He's such a special little boy, our grandson. It's interesting the things that go through children's heads. He loves our apartment because it's so big, but he was afraid to be too far away from me. And he asked very tenderly if I missed you, if I was lonely in the big apartment all by myself. Last December, when his baby sister was having trouble breathing and was rushed to the hospital and I was staying with him, he told me about his fears. He said he was afraid of dying. I told him how, when your mom had died, and then mine, and you had been so ill, how I had been afraid. How not a day had passed then without my thinking about death and dying, and my heart would palpitate so fast. And then, it went away. I don't know how or why, but one day the thoughts, the palpitations just weren't there.

Then he told me he was also afraid of going blind. And I asked him where that was coming from, and he explained that one day at school they brought in a blind lady and her eyes had been so funny, so strange. It made him terribly afraid. And then he said, "They shouldn't do that with little kids—we're too young—it's scary. We don't understand, and I'm a very sensitive boy."

As they say, out of the mouths of babes.

Los Angeles, October 12, 1992

My darling Norman, my beautiful love,

Today I've done something I've never done before. I canceled a trip because I was feeling ill!

They were supposed to pick me up at 11:30 a.m. and by 9:30 I was diagnosing everything from stress to heart attack. (You remember how good I am at diagnosing illnesses—like the time you were having the gall bladder attack that led to emergency surgery and I was diagnosing "psychosomatic" stress.)

So this time I was doing the opposite, figuring "heart attack," when it probably was nerves or maybe a stomach virus. But I've had a strange pain in the left side of my chest for a few weeks now, and my father was just a year older than me when he died. So when the nausea, biliousness, cold sweat and diarrhea set in, "heart attack" didn't seem too farfetched or melodramatic.

Of course, the sharp stomach pains could just mean my thyroid is acting up again. But, enough was wrong that I called my doctor (and you know how unusual that is for me).

As luck would have it, he was out of town, and the thought of having a heart attack with strangers in attendance didn't appeal. I thought of calling your cardiologist, Dr. Charuzi, but I was afraid he would feel compelled to call me in for all sorts of tests and examinations. (And what if he found something? I had to go back to work in Toronto and there was no way I wasn't going to do that.) Besides, all I was really looking for was someone to tell me, "It's nothing, it'll go away."

So I decided I wasn't going to have a heart attack just then, but the thought of having to drag myself through an airport and get on a plane was more than I could bear. I changed my flight to tomorrow at the crack of dawn—but that gives me time to feel better.

This trip home has reminded me why it was always such a relief for us, especially you, to get out of town. I remembered how we'd sit down in the plane and we could feel the weight falling off our shoulders. Ellen said to me the other day, "I bet you can't wait to get out of here!"

Everybody's life in L.A. is just falling apart. Well, maybe not everybody's, but those close to me. Mark is in all kinds of trouble. Lauren has separated. Rochelle is going to a sanitarium. Bobbi and Al are under all kinds of pressure, and the air is so bad, so smoggy, it makes the atmospheric conditions depicted in *Soylent Green* seem desirable. In fact, the only difference is that in the movie they had the good sense to wear oxygen masks. Here we're still pretending smog doesn't exist. And Bobbi wants to know why I don't want to live here!

I've decided I'm going to try and stay put in Toronto for the next couple of weeks. I realize I've been running a lot. Running to fill the days. Running to fill the nights. Running to fill the time. Running because I don't want a world without you in it! And when I stop running, I have to face that fact.

God, I don't want a world without you in it! *I don't want a world without you in it!* What am I going to do in a world without you in it?

On one of my last visits to the cemetery I was sitting on the grass right by your grave and, as I looked up through my tears at the expanse of plaques imbedded on the rolling hillside, my gaze came to rest on a white-haired woman sitting on a bench under a tree at the top of the hill, framed against the sky. She must have been more than 100 feet away so I couldn't see her face, but I could tell she wasn't crying. She just sat there, peacefully, staring out at nothing in particular. Or perhaps conversing silently with the one she loved—as if she had always been there and would stay until the day she died. I watched her and wondered if that was going to be me 10, 20, 30...100 years from now.

It was a difficult Yom Kippur. More than sitting and atoning for my sins—I sat and mourned that you were not there with me and the tears streamed down my face and I could not stop them, except when we kibitzed—Philip, Ellen and I—to try and hide our pain.

As I entered the synagogue that night and saw the candles burning, I realized I had forgotten to light mine. When I asked Philip about it, he said he thought it was just on the *yahrzeits* that you lit candles. But I remembered the five candles you used to light all together—the ones for your mother, father and stepfather, and one each for my mom and dad. And I smiled as I remembered the year my mother's candle wouldn't stay lit until we separated her from the pack. Ever the snob! How we laughed. Anyway, I told Philip that with you gone, all our

"Jewishness," the customs, the heritage, the memories, everything is going out the window! Without you, we're just a bunch of heathens.

I never doubted that my mother's presence could a flickering candle make, and I smiled, remembering that we had both immediately and independently assumed that the temperamental one was my mother's candle! And the memory took me back to her time in the hospital.

Sometimes when people tell me I have to let go of you, I can't help wondering again why I get so few messages from you—what's holding you back? Why don't you communicate? Is it because you know if you came to me, that would fill my days and my nights and I wouldn't ever need, or want, anything or anybody else?

I am, after all, receptive. Cancers are naturally psychic. Do you remember how the messages about my mother came through so loud and clear?

I remember everything about that time so vividly. Getting the message in the office that she had collapsed in her room, urging them to call the paramedics, calling you to meet me at Cedars. And I remember being with her in the emergency room, as she lay, unable to speak because of the stroke that had paralyzed her on one side. But her eyes were alert and expressive, only she went downhill from there.

I remember, weeks before that day, getting a call from the retirement hotel when she couldn't remember, or couldn't dial, our phone number. I picked her up and she was okay but had obviously had a minor stroke—like the one she had fully recovered from four years earlier. Now she couldn't articulate the words she had in her head.

And some things she couldn't remember at all.

We were about to leave for New York on an assignment I had for Norman Lear, and I made provisions for Jeff's mother to be with her every day to make sure she didn't forget to eat or dress, or anything like that.

When we got back a week later I had the limo driver pick her up and bring her to the airport to meet us and on that hot March day she was wearing her black mink. I said to you as we exited the terminal, "Why is she wearing a fur coat?" And when I asked her, she only replied, "I'm glad you'll have this from me."

The next day I was on my way over to her, but I called and told her I needed to stop in my office first. She was disoriented and started to cry because she was so frustrated that she couldn't find anything. I tried to soothe her but she was inconsolable, and I promised to be there as soon as I could. And then in the office that phone call came.

In the hospital the ordeal began. The tests she didn't want to take. The dreaded CAT scan, which frightened her so, although I could never understand why. And the battery of things they did. Later I wondered what for, since aspirin seemed to be all they were administering. Because she couldn't talk, I arranged for round-the-clock help—in the daytime, a Russian refugee lady I was hoping she would warm up to, and at night, Comfort Adoma (I can't believe I still remember her name!) the young black nurse from Africa.

As my mother deteriorated, I felt more helpless. I vacillated between anger that they weren't doing anything to rehabilitate her and resignation that made me give instructions for "no heroic measures." My God, how many mixed messages!

And dear and wonderful friends, like Dan Birman, who came and spent hours every day talking to her, trying to help her keep her grip on reality. And me, bringing work to the hospital, sitting there talking to her about taking trips and going to Europe. I remember one afternoon, she actually laughed—or was it a sneer?—when I was talking like that. Because she knew she wasn't going anywhere. Certainly not in the state she was in. It reminded me of the time when she was trying to talk to me about her eventual death. I changed the subject, and she accused me of talking about going to Europe when she was talking about dying!

Now, as I think back on that, I know she was right. We should have talked, but I could never deal with the thought of her death. I guess I felt talking about it would make me seem callous somehow. I just couldn't, but I should have, even if it brought me pain. Now I realize I was denying her, just like so many people in my life had ignored my feelings in so many ways.

Slowly she slipped further and further away. By the end of the week, she was tossing and turning and I was sure she was in pain. All those insensitive doctors would say is that people who've had strokes don't feel pain. How the hell do they know that?!

So, in desperation, knowing I had to find a way to get through to her, I called my friend Joan Thornton, who traveled in psychic circles. She gave me the phone number of someone she knew. I called and he talked to me at length and said he didn't feel that my mother was in any kind of pain. In the course of the conversation he said to me, "You know, there's a very strong bond between a parent and a child, and sometimes you have to let go."

I didn't pay much attention to that because it was her pain I was concerned with and he had made me feel better. But that was Friday. By Saturday she was worse. I banned all the technicians from her room and said, no, they couldn't have any more blood because she wasn't some research experiment. All those blood-sucking tests weren't resulting in any kind of medication being prescribed or treatment being administered or anything that was making her get any better.

The doctors were telling us this could go on for a very long time, so I started making preparations to take her to our home. They were against that. They thought we should be looking into a nursing home because of her "handicap." But she had no handicap. They had her hooked up to a urine bag (I still don't know why that was necessary), but even if that needed to be done—what was so difficult? We could get a nurse to come in.

After all, you and I were working with and knew about a lot of severely disabled people, and they were managing. I remembered one film about a guy up north who was strapped to a stretcher and controlled the motor mechanism with his teeth. He used to go out alone, for God's sake, on the streets of San Francisco. Why was the medical profession so against my taking one frail, partially paralyzed woman home?

By Sunday, my mother seemed to be tossing and turning even more and I was a basket case. I called Joan again and she told me about a friend of hers who was a psychologist/hypnotist who worked with patients at UCLA on handling pain and dying. His name was Hal Rogers and she thought he might be in his office that day. After I called him, that wonderful, gentle, kind man volunteered to come to the hospital that evening.

He sat in the quiet waiting room not far from my mother's room and talked to us for more than an hour. Actually, he mostly listened as we answered the questions he posed. Finally, he said, "It's very clear from what you've told me that your mother would not want to live as an invalid, paralyzed and confined to her bed." I concurred. My mother's idea of "dependence" was when I sent a chauffeured limousine to pick her up! She hated it. I used to tell her I wish someone would do that for me, but that did not change her mind. If she couldn't be independent, she couldn't be free!

Hal Rogers continued in his soft, soothing voice, "You know, at times, parents need permission from their children to leave. Their time has come, but the child won't release the parent. Sometimes you have to let go."

As tears filled my eyes, I told Dr. Rogers that I could not just go in and tell my mother it was okay for her to die. I just couldn't do that. He nodded and said, "But I can—if you want me to."

You and I looked at each other, then I nodded to him, unable to speak, and he disappeared behind her closed door and you held me tight in your arms.

Finally, after what seemed to be a very long time (but was probably only 10 or 20 minutes), he came out and said she was resting peacefully. We went in, said goodnight and went home.

On Monday evening when I got to the hospital, the nurse Comfort, who had had the weekend off, asked if she could speak to me. I followed her into the hall and this dear, sensitive, young woman began to tell me a story—about how sick her father had become just before she was to leave Africa to come to the States. And how she had kept postponing her trip, and her father kept hanging on. Finally she had realized that she must go and he had died a couple of weeks later. And then she said to me that the hospital didn't care who was lying in that bed. They didn't care about my mother—only the money they made every time someone walked into that room. She thought my mother was in terrible pain. And she said to me, "There comes a time when a child has to let a parent go."

I looked up to Heaven and said in my head, "Okay, I hear you. The message is coming through loud and clear."

I thanked Comfort and went in to my mother, stroked her hair and said, "Mommy, I don't want to see you like this—and it's okay." That night, as I took off my make-up, I looked into the mirror and said, "Daddy, come and get her. She should not have to suffer like this."

And my mother died peacefully the following day.

When I went to a psychic not long after, she told me my mother was happy and free and was holding hands with a man she called "Willy." My father's Anglicized name was William—something the psychic could not have known in a million years.

❧ ～ ❧

In the dentist's office the other day (dental work is one of the reasons I've been flying back and forth from Toronto so frequently), I picked up a *New Yorker* and couldn't believe what I saw:

"A minute ago
I was locked in my room
My life seemed pointless and hollow,
Where before it was warm
With the presence of Norm,
And I thought, 'Where he's gone I must follow.'
I looked at the Valium, I considered the stove,
I weighed up the stern moral issues.
But the strength inside me grew
When I was almost through
My last box of Kleenex tissues.
So I hope you'll applaud my great achievement.
I am here tonight in spite of my bereavement..."

I take everything that happens to me, or falls into my hands, as having special meaning. Messages from the other side. I will grasp at anything. So I decided that was you telling me suicide was not an option.

The poem was part of an article about an English entertainer known as Dame Edna making "her" comeback appearance at the Drury Lane Theatre in March of 1989. She's the creation of Barry Humphries and has taken on a life of her own. "Norm" is her fictitious spouse—who also took on a presence of his own without ever appearing on the stage.

Of course, she's a comic figure and some people took umbrage at her mockery of bereavement. But I take everything at face value these days, and try to read deep meaning into everything that crosses my path.

That same issue of the *New Yorker* had an ad for a "Chocolate Fantasy Cruise" on the *QE2* sponsored by Nestle! Had you known of it, you would have booked us on that one for sure!

Last August there was a small article in the financial section of the newspaper. It was about a settlement in the class action suit against the manufacturers of the defective valves. They were accused of knowing the valves could fracture and result in possible death. Under the settlement they have to provide $75 million for any needed valve replacement surgeries and to pay for research to identify other valve users who may be at risk.

I wondered whimsically if we could have been part of the class action suit, charging "extenuating circumstances due to death as a result of fear."

I'm finishing this letter on the plane and we're on the approach to Toronto. In the distance the downtown skyscrapers and the Needle seem like they could fit in the palm of my hand. It's a beautiful, clear day and it really looks like you can see forever.

I brought back one of the greeting cards you gave me. I place all these mementos around the apartment, next to pictures of you. They keep me company and keep you close to me.

This one's a Blue Mountain Arts card by Nanci Brillant. On the cover you've written, "Dearest Fern," and the card goes on to say:

I'm so lucky to have found you

On the inside, it says:

Once in a lifetime,
You find someone,
who touches not only your heart,
but also your soul.
Once in a lifetime,
you discover someone
who stands beside you, not over you.
You find someone
who loves you for who you are,
and not for who you could be.
Once in a lifetime,
if you're lucky,
you find someone...
as I have found you.

You signed it, "Your Normele." I feel that way, too.

My beloved,

I've just finished writing to Dr. Charuzi about the Save a Heart Foundation Cardiac Research Fellowship I'm establishing in your name. It's been a good year and it's time to give back in some small way. Who knows? Maybe a recipient will make some incredible breakthrough and we'll have helped someone else with your heart condition to live a few more years.

I'm also establishing a film finishing grant in both our names through the Women In Film Foundation for projects having to do with the environment. When I was last in L.A., I never got to see the city—the smog was that bad! We've got to do something! We just can't sit by and let our world self-destruct this way.

When I finished writing the letter to Charuzi, I got up from my desk and walked to the bay windows, which give a 180-degree view of the city and the lake from my downtown Toronto apartment. And Normy, it was the most incredible sunset! How we would have loved watching it together. You with your arms around me and our bodies close together gazing at the wondrous world we live in. How can anybody not do everything they can to preserve that kind of beauty?

It had been a crystal clear day—the buildings stood out against the cobalt blue sky and the puffy white clouds hung like cotton candy on high. And then, as the sun began to set, the hues of pink and red set in. By the time I walked over to the windows, there was an incredible band of red on the horizon blending into an iridescent blue, which was turning into a midnight sky. And in the middle of it all, amidst the twinkling lights of landing planes, one light hung out over the water—the first star in the night sky. I made a wish and watched with wonder as the colors deepened, turning into darker lavenders and purples and I became aware of the sounds of celebration drifting through the air.

Toronto won the World Series yesterday. They played the Atlanta Braves, and coincidentally, your old friend Graham Cole called me from there to say hello last night.

You can imagine the revelry that's going on here in the streets—brisk fall weather notwithstanding. Not only is it the first time the Blue Jays have played in the World Series, but they won! The only thing that would have been better for them would have been to win on their own home turf. Then the place really would have gone berserk. Anyway, isn't it interesting that we always called it the "World Series" but we never played with anyone but ourselves? Until now. Seems a little arrogant, don't you think? (On the other hand, it's also a little ironic that there isn't one Canadian on the Blue Jays team! I just heard that on the radio this morning and was truly stunned.)

Yesterday, too, I had my first Toronto party. It was an "open house" and I had invited about 60 people—40 showed up. (You know me, I had to sit down right after the party and see who had actually come. Only there was no one doing it with me, and no one to talk to about the guests!)

It was a good party, all very nice, except for the caterer I had selected, who calls himself Gordon W. He had been recommended by a couple of people from the office and turned out to be a disaster—although nobody really knew it except me. But I was really angry!

Can you imagine? The bartender and part of the food arrived only 10 minutes before I expected the first guests! And the rest of the food arrived two hours later—for a party that was only scheduled to last four hours! He also lied about coming over himself. His people had a real attitude and were so clumsy they broke more things in one evening than at all the parties we've ever given all over the world. (The guests *did* notice that.) And, he also charged more than the estimate—but since I still had people around when the help left, I didn't argue. Life is too short and it's only money. But you know he's not getting any recommendations from me. Quite the contrary—if I ever hear his name mentioned!

The sunset tonight reminded me of an evening last summer in Paris at EuroDisney. An actor friend of René and Albert Hague, Dorothy Constantine, called me. Her husband was appearing as Buffalo Bill in the *Wild West Show*, and she had just been asked to do Diamond Lil in another revue. So they weren't able to come to Paris and visit, but they extended an invitation to come see the show. So I took Nina Rosenthal and it really was a treat. The theater is set up like a giant horseshoe with counters and benches, and they serve a "ranch-style" dinner during the show. Barbecue chicken and ribs, chili, corn, etc. It was delicious and plentiful. You would've enjoyed it. And the revue was very entertaining, too.

When we walked out after the show, it was still quite light—you know how late the sun sets on a summer night in Paris. I remember, years ago, having a heated argument with my mother when she said it stays lighter longer in Europe. I was young and couldn't imagine how that could be. If she had only said, "Because it's further north, dummy!" I would have understood. But she didn't, and I was stubborn, so it just deteriorated into one of those child-parent arguments that goes on forever. Sorry, Ma—you were right again!

Anyway, the sun was just setting and the sky was pink and purple and the Disney hotels, with all their fairy-tale lights, twinkled against the sky like a million stars—looking like a version of the Arabian Nights. It was truly magical and I missed you so.

I imagined again how we would have stood and reveled in the beauty surrounding us. I could feel how your strong arms would have enveloped me as you held me close with my back pressing against your strong, battle-scarred chest. I would feel the warmth of your body against mine, and your love would encompass me—surrounding me with an aura of well-being, and the love that I miss so much.

I realized the other night I don't feel as "needy" as I did right after you died! God how I longed to feel strong arms around me. I was sometimes embarrassed because my need felt so great I thought surely people could hear my cravings, my thoughts crying out, "Please, put your arms around me! Hold me, hug me tight. I need to feel the warmth of another body, another human being. Oh, please, somebody—anybody—just hold me tight."

Fortunately, every time I saw Michael and Gloria, they would do just that—especially Michael who would envelop me in one of his big bear hugs that are so much like yours and I would tell him how much I needed it, only I'm not sure he knew how much I really meant what I was saying.

I even wondered, thought about, what a lesbian relationship might be like. There are a lot of great women out there. But I've come to the conclusion that that's just not in the cards for me. I've loved men all my life—too much, too long, for too many years to change now. And ever since I can remember, I've had interesting, challenging men in my life. So, if I don't find another one now, I'll just fill my life with the ones I've had—either in person, or in my head. (Simon's right. That is where I'm living. Do you think there's something wrong with that?)

Edith Taylor, who came to do some work for me the other day, told me about a friend of hers who's widowed and doesn't have one picture of her late husband around because she says it hurts too much. I'm just the opposite. Your pictures are everywhere. You smile at me wherever I look, keeping me company and giving me comfort. And the little love notes you always left for me in unexpected places are all over the apartment and the office. You're with me.

It's when I think of putting away the pictures, saying it's over and time to get on with the rest of my life, that the pain and panic set in. It's the thought of wiping you out of my life that frightens me.

There's a song out there titled, "How Am I Supposed To Live Without You?" Some of the lyrics echo so much of what I feel. "How can I go on living without you, after I've been loving you so long? How am I supposed to carry on, when all that I've been living for is gone?"

You've even started popping up in my dreams a little more frequently—though not nearly as vividly, or as much as I would like, or had expected.

I remember the first time you came to me in a dream. I was very unhappy with what was going on at work, and one night I dreamt I was riding in a big limousine. White, maybe. As we headed down an L.A. street we crossed an intersection and were approaching a bus stop where a number of people were waiting for the bus. You were standing in front of the crowd and smiling at the limousine, even though it had smoked windows so there's no way you could have seen me in there. As we came abreast of you, I rolled down the window, smiled and offered you a lift. You got in, sat down, looked at me, smiled and said, "So what's the matter? What's so terrible? Why are you so sad?"

I don't remember anymore, but when I woke up the next morning, I remembered dreaming of you and I didn't feel quite so bad.

Sometime last year I saw a rerun of a *Golden Girls* episode that was basically about one of Blanche's dreams in which her husband isn't really dead. When she wakes up and realizes it was her recurring dream again, she tells Dorothy it's okay now. Because this time she didn't wake up until after he had hugged her and told her he had forgiven her for something, or that he understood about something. I can't quite remember which it was, but I need you to do that with me.

I need to have you come and hold me, hug me and tell me that you didn't go because you couldn't face the thought of what the future might bring. I know you were jealous of the time I spent away from you, jealous of the people that surrounded me and the exhilaration I was feeling because of the challenge of the work in that first year of *Counterstrike*.

And because you were so much in love with me, you thought every man who met me would fall in love with me, too. We never talked about it, but you knew that I knew that you knew. For the first time in our relationship, I think you felt threatened.

On the plane the other day, there was a short article about a man who had an automobile accident and a near-death experience. It's entitled "I Chose Life." It tells about his floating over everything and watching himself lying on the hospital bed, and then being pulled in two directions. But finally, his will to live was stronger than his desire for the peace and freedom he felt while "bathed in the light." He talks about being "in control" that day—and how he "chose life." And, even before reading that article, I've often wondered what you saw that night as your body lay struggling for breath and I was calling the paramedics—and why you didn't choose life.

≈ ∼ ≈

The CD player has just switched to Pavarotti in his performance with Domingo and Carreras at Terme di Caracalla—the performance I saw on PBS the night of your birthday in '91.

The song is "Memory" from *Cats* and "it's so easy to leave me" echoes through the air. Was it easy for you to leave me?

The music reminds me of a lovely performance I attended a few weeks ago at Radio City Music Hall.

Jim McManus gave a special cocktail party preceding a performance of Michael Crawford singing Andrew Lloyd Webber's music. As with all the events that Jim hosts, it was exquisite. Cocktails were served on the mezzanine and, of course, the ambiance at the Music Hall was extraordinary. The hors d'oeuvres were fantastic, and the performance was fabulous. Crawford and the cast were terrific—it was a really memorable evening.

I invited Arthur Weingarten, who happened to be in New York, to join me. Remember him from my days at Tandem? He dated Kelly Smith, but they broke up and he's now married to a very lovely Australian actress,

Annette Andre, and they live in London and L.A. He was impressed because Jim and Eileen had reserved seats for me right next to them and we really had a good time.

It was interesting for me to see how I responded when I was introducing Arthur to Jim and Eileen. Suddenly I felt this strong need to make it perfectly clear that Arthur was only a friend, not a date. So I think the introduction went something like, "Jim, Eileen, I'd like you to meet Arthur Weingarten, an old friend. We used to work together for Norman Lear. His wife is in London and he's here for a few days." I may be exaggerating a little, and I don't think anyone really noticed—but I did.

The funny thing is, Arthur is exactly the kind of man I would love to go out with because we have so much in common and he makes me laugh. He's bright, he's easy to talk to and be with—and yet I was uncomfortable that our friends might think I was "dating" someone, that he might be replacing you after only a little over a year.

And during the holidays at a temple benefit performance to which I had ordered extra tickets, I noted that I chose to go alone. It's almost as if I was wearing my "aloneness" like a badge. The empty chair next to me represented you.

At Jim's cocktail party, as I looked down at the crowd of theater-goers filling up the Music Hall's extraordinary Art Deco main lobby, I remembered our many visits there with our "pink suitcase" full of Chantal Goya's records and cassettes of Jean-Jacques Debout's *The Mysterious Voyage of Marie-Rose,* as we pitched the project to Jim and his staff. And later, as I sat in the darkened theater, I remembered how many truly special moments we've shared with Jim and Eileen as a result of those French children's mega-musicals we were so keen to produce.

None of us will ever forget the weekend at Chantal and Jean-Jacques' various castles in France. And the fabulous dinner parties Jim gave for them in the fabled private suites of Rockefeller Center when they were in New York. If we ever launch the English-version stage productions of those fabulous shows, they will all be dedicated to you—because we all love you so much.

Toronto, November 8, 1992

Normy, my darling, my love,

Jacques Brel is singing "Ne Me Quittez Pas" on the CD player and the clouds have covered the sun that was shining brilliantly just minutes ago. The tears hover in my eyes about to spill over as I listen to the words that meant so much to us then—when we first met—and now, since you've gone away.

It reminds me of another day, another time, so many years ago when you had gone away and I was alone...

Parting

It's night now and I'm alone
with my thoughts.
Your face looks out at me from the television set
as an actor's gesture becomes your embrace.
Two make-believe lovers kiss and my whole
body feels the warmth of your embrace—
And longs for your closeness.
It helped that you left in the morning,
the day was not hard to bear.
But it's night now and sleep—unlike other nights—
is very far away.
The quiet—so often longed for and enjoyed—is
empty now, devoid of all but desolation.
The laughter—so lightly taken and accepted—
rings mockingly in my ears
Emphasizing its absence.

The comfort of your arms is gone—
alive only in memory.
Your tender glance, your warm caress,
Your love—are all so far away.
You love me—I know that now and more
each passing day.
That makes it harder—and harder still—
each time you go away.
I sit here—alone now—and write to you
while a slow ache grows within—
Till it twists and turns and my whole being
burns to have you here with me.
Not just to hold you and feel you close
and have you deep within me—
But to see your love and to bask in the glow
of something so full of good feeling.
But you're gone now and I sit here alone
With only my thoughts and my feelings.

(*Ne me quittez pas...ne me quittez pas...*why did you go away?)

This morning as I opened my eyes the world outside seemed shrouded in a white fog. It was early so I turned over for another half-hour. The next time I looked I realized it was snowing! And by the time I got up there was a white blanket on all the roofs and the streets of the city.

It reminded me of the time we drove up to Lake Louise from Calgary when I was doing *Mr. Wizard's*

World. It was a lovely, sunny morning when we left the city and drove into those breathtaking Canadian Rockies and checked into the Chateau. The next morning—Mother's Day and our wedding anniversary—we awoke to a winter wonderland. The snow drifted down silently in flakes as big as cotton puffs. We grinned at each other as you took me in your arms, and it was as if God had given us a beautiful anniversary present, totally unexpected and full of wonder. Remember?

Last September ('91) when I wrote to our friends to watch the second season premiere of *Counterstrike* on USA, I started by telling them:

> *"It's me again, bringing you up-to-date on where I am, and how. Hard to believe it's mid-September already. Where has the summer gone?*
>
> *I'm okay. Some things get easier—a lot of things get harder—like a cloudless summer day, or an excruciatingly beautiful sunset—and Norman isn't there to share it with me. Yes, I know he's watching from another dimension. I'd like it better if he were watching it from this one, with me.*
>
> *Your phone calls, letters, and notes (which I am still answering one by one—bear with me) continue to bring me solace. Just when I'm at my lowest there will be a call from Sydney, or Paris or L.A. I only hope I can give to each and every one of you as much love and support as you've given me this past year."*

Then I went on to give them details of the show's air dates—and my addresses. People tease me that they have whole pages of phone numbers and addresses for me. I laugh and tell them to write it all in pencil, which is the way I do my life—in pencil!

This year I wrote them about a special episode that kicked off our third season. The letter started out like this:

Dear Friends,

Here I am back in Toronto after a glorious time in 'gay Paree' where we shot 14 episodes of Counterstrike.

Our third season premiere episode is one we're particularly proud of. Not only does it include Christopher Plummer improvising at the keyboard (I had no idea he could play the piano so well)—but as the title 'Cherchez La Femme' indicates, it has Peter Sinclair (played by Simon MacCorkindale) on the trail of a woman who has made more of an impact on him than he cares to admit.

Meanwhile, Alexander Addington (Christopher Plummer's character) is beginning to come to terms with the fact that his 'period of mourning' (for his kidnapped wife) must come to an end—something I can relate to only too well. So, while Alexander is opening himself up to the attraction he feels for his executive assistant, Helene Previn, Peter is losing someone he could have loved. It's a situation which draws the two men closer together and strengthens the bond of friendship they already feel for each other.

And, while it's true that I can relate to Alexander's need to put his "period of mourning" behind him, unfortunately, I haven't found the male equivalent of Helene Previn to fill the void. But the episode has a special place in my heart for another reason. In a scene between Helene and Alexander, I was able to memorialize forever (or at least, for as long as the reruns last) a philosophy that you and I so often shared.

In the scene, Alexander has just learned that a business associate has caused his bank considerable grief by trying to hide funds from his wife due to their impending divorce. Alexander turns to Helene and tells her that love has been the cause of more trouble in the world than anyone can imagine. Helene (who is a widow) disagrees. She says, "On the contrary, Mr. Addington, my husband and I used to say that love is the force of life."

Alexander looks at her, perhaps seeing her for the very first time, and raises his glass in a toast, "To life, Ms. Previn." She smiles at him and does the same. And every time they raise their glasses, that toast, my darling, is for you. "To life!"

This year I was at home in L.A. for our anniversary. The anniversary of our meeting, that is. In fact, I drove down to the desert to check out our condo before the seasonal rentals begin. (I've been resorting to that since it fell out of escrow.)

Beverly Raymond, who worked for us at Brookfield ages ago, rode down with me. She is staying in the apartment in Marina del Rey to help me try to get organized while she figures out where she's going to spend the rest of her life. Incidentally, this time L.A. was magnificent.

I could see way beyond the Hollywood sign every day from our windows—especially from your loft/office.

Down in the desert, it was incredible. Clear, and crisp, and beautiful. All the reasons why we bought down there. The mountains sparkled against the blue sky and when the sun set, the pinks and purples glowed warmly as the last daylight disappeared, and a million stars came out, and how I missed you!

I had enough to do in the condo—or maybe I looked for things to keep me busy—so that I couldn't just sit around and absorb the beauty of it all. But that day, October 31, 1992, it was all there.

Our gardener, Kathy Hudson, came by to say hello and to take down a few scorched leaves, which she said always annoyed you so. The courtyard looked good and the kumquat tree (the first one we planted) is really getting big. But the two ficus trees have died and those little plants that lead up to the front door are in arrested development. I swear they haven't grown an inch in 10 years! It's hard to believe, but that's what it's been since we bought the place—10 years!

I told her to replace the two trees that died because it looks very bare on the left side of the courtyard, and I'm putting down more gravel in the front area where the ground cover never seems to last. It probably won't make any difference in the sale of the place. But it does still belong to us and, as long as that's so, I want it to reflect what it was when we lived there.

The desk in the den is a mess. It has cracked in what almost looks like a marble pattern that matches that floor lamp you love so much. I'm sure Gates Refinishing doesn't want to hear from me anymore. And the realtor said to forget about it, but I can't. (You know how I love things to be perfect.) They simply put too many coats of paint on it—and I guess it cracked because it got so hot in the desert this year.

The place, my darling, the first home I ever owned, the first place we decorated together, still has such good vibes, my sweet husband. All the love we put into fixing it up is still there, bouncing from the rafters. It's a happy place with lots of good memories. Every piece in the house represents a special moment in our life together—good times, times when we picked things out.

Remember how we used to kid about the fact that we liked the same things? We would both be drawn to something in a store and then one of us would start to rant and rave that we couldn't go on like that—always wanting the same things, liking the same things, never disagreeing. And then we would laugh and think of people we knew who couldn't agree on anything. How lucky we were, my darling. How many marriages and relationships come to the brink of destruction over simple things, because the partners simply can't agree. And how important those disagreements can seem, how large they loom when you're young. I remember those times, those arguments—in other relationships and other places.

By the time Beverly and I got back to L.A., it was late and I didn't have much time to contemplate the passing of the 25th anniversary of our first meeting. But I remember it now.

It was Halloween, 1967. I was living with Konny (actually "married to" but looking to get out) on Sutton Place, and working with him in his industrial film company. We came home that night tired and cranky as usual, and were supposed to have dinner with my uncle Dave and cousins Bob and Sylvin. We had talked about going to the theater, but no one had been able to get tickets to anything we all wanted to see. So Dave suggested I pick a restaurant—dinner was on him.

I don't know why—maybe I thought my uncle would like to go back to his ethnic roots—but I picked the Russian Bear and we agreed to pick him up at the Regency and go on from there.

When we got home, Konny wasn't feeling well. But then that was nothing new in our life. With him you never knew if it was physical or a manifestation of his depressions and mood swings. There were so many weekends that he spent just lying in bed, while I wallowed in my guilt, never realizing on a gut level that his feelings of depression had very little to do with me.

He was dragging himself around getting dressed when he finally sat down and said he really didn't feel like going but knew if he didn't, he would never hear the end of it. I said, "Wrong. If you go and make everybody's life miserable, you'll never hear the end of it." So he said he really didn't feel up to it and I said I would go by myself.

When I was a little girl and feeling bored or unhappy, my mother always used to say to me, "Fernandina, you never know what the day will bring." She was right. How different all our lives might have been if Konny had gone to dinner that night!

I don't know why I took the VW van instead of the Jag, because now that I think of it, we surely would all have fit into the sedan. Anyway, I opted for the van with the Marathon International logo emblazoned on its side. So, there I was in my black velvet trench coat, shimmery cocktail dress, stiletto heels, and sequined hat covering the hair I had not had time to wash or fix, driving up to the Regency where my uncle was already having an argument with the doorman.

Nothing new or unusual in that either. Everybody in my family was a type-A personality with little or no tolerance for perceived incompetence of any kind. Which means they went around fighting with the world. Of course, they were also all brilliant and successful, and could be extremely charming. And I was invariably attracted to people who were just like that.

When Dave got into the van he told me Bob (my cousin Lilyan's husband—his son-in-law) and a friend of the family who was also in town on business, were waiting for us at the Plaza Hotel. Sylvin, his son, was late as usual, and would meet us at the Russian Bear.

I remember the first time I saw you, standing next to Bob on the steps of the Plaza Hotel.

You were gorgeous. You had auburn hair, a red goatee and moustache (which instantly reminded me of Aldo). You were built like a big teddy bear (which reminded me of Aldo and Julie) and I remember thinking, "How come my family knows somebody who looks as interesting as that? He should be wearing a beret and a turtleneck sweater, and be painting in a Parisian garret on the Left Bank."

And, I didn't know it then, but you were already hooked on me.

Apparently, my reputation as the black sheep of the family had preceded me and you had already decided I was some sort of fabulous "femme fatale" you were eager to meet. I can just imagine what my family must have told you about me—divorced, living in sin (actually by then Konny and I were married, but I hadn't really told anybody) and I had lived alone in Rome during the time of La Dolce Vita! I could have looked like a gorilla and you still would have been intrigued. Luckily, I didn't.

I remember smiling to myself as I could see Cousin Bob cringe at having to get into a van with advertising splattered across its side, right in front of the elegant Plaza Hotel. But you both got in and introductions were made. The restaurant wasn't far, and fortunately there was a garage right across the street. As we walked up the driveway, you cavalierly took me by the arm and I noted your firm, but gentle touch. Many months later you told me as soon as you touched my elbow, "chills ran up and down your spine" and I got "under your skin."

Dinner was a disaster. There wasn't another soul in the restaurant, and no one came in the whole night either. Bob had a bad cold and was rapidly fading. By the time Sylvin arrived his father was so furious with him you could cut the tension with a knife. And, in the middle of all this, the waiter was so rude he made the legendary ones at Sardi's—or was it Lindy's?—seem like they were graduates of Miss Manners.

I sat there thanking my lucky stars that Konny had not come with us, because there's no question he and the waiter would have come to blows. And there you were—

making light of every situation, making jokes, making even my uncle smile, and saving what could have been a debacle.

I couldn't get over it—how you diffused every volatile situation. With Konny we couldn't go to a movie that he wouldn't fight with the usher, the cashier, the person sitting next to us, and here you were taking potentially disastrous situations and turning them benign. I hadn't relaxed like that in years.

And, of course, we did flirt with our eyes across the table, but we—or at least I—couldn't be blatant about it, because I was, after all, a married woman. And I had no idea about you—but you were a "friend of the family!"

When dinner was finally over my uncle said he was sure that I wanted to get back to my sick husband, so we dropped Dave off first at the Regency, and then headed for the Plaza, although Sylvin had suggested we go meet some of his friends for a drink. Bob said he wasn't feeling up to it and as we pulled up to the hotel he asked if you were coming in. You said no, you'd go have a drink with Sylvin and Fern, and Bob said, "I thought so." I guess he must have seen what was happening. Our looks had not been as discreet as they might have been.

So we went to some hotel bar on the East Side in the 30s (was it called The Carriage House?), and then you asked me if I'd like to go someplace quiet for a drink. I said not a drink, but coffee would be fine. So we left Sylvin and his friends and the only place we could find for coffee was the old Horn & Hardart on 42nd and Third and as you went to get the coffee I agonized how to find out if you were married—because all through dinner I had kept wondering if you were the Prince Charming who was going to rescue me from the misery that I was in. But, of course, if you were married then you couldn't be the one. And because you were a friend of my family, and I was not free, I didn't want to seem obvious and just ask you straight out. Finally, I found the question that I thought would tell me what I needed to know without letting you know that I was really interested in you.

"Do you have any children?" I asked, and held my breath, as you sat down beside me juggling the cups of coffee in your elegant hands. "Three," you answered candidly, as my heart sank to my toes and I said goodbye to my knight in shining armor.

I don't remember much of the conversation after that. I know you told me you traveled a lot for business, did a lot of things on your own (the theater, dinners, etc.) when you were on the road, which for someone like me—who had never done anything alone—seemed strange and lonely. And there was also a part of me, the cynic, that didn't believe a word of it—not for a minute. Alone? Not someone as good-looking and interesting as you!

And I told you some superficial things about my life. But as far as I was concerned, it didn't matter because I was never going to see you again.

As we walked out to the van we kibitzed and laughed and you offered to accompany me home and take a cab from Sutton Place, but I said that was absolutely unnecessary. I explained to you that I drove all over the city at all hours of the night. It didn't bother me. It was okay.

You were a little surprised. You weren't used to that kind of absence of fear—especially in a woman.

(What I didn't tell you then was that I was always storming out of the house in the middle of the night after some violent argument with Konny, and either walking or driving the streets of Manhattan trying to cool down. I would eventually tell you—but that was to come much later.)

So that night, as we drove back to the Plaza we made small talk. You asked me about various places around the city (restaurants, clubs, etc.) and I hadn't been to any of them! Finally you laughed and said, "Maybe the next time I come into town, you'll let me show you *my* New York." And I said, "Yeah, yeah, sure." For me, it was over—before anything had even begun. You had your family and your life, and I was looking for mine in the middle of the nightmare I was living and you were clearly not my saviour, and would not play a part in it.

Little did I know...

So, you see, my mother was right. You never know what the day will bring. I had no idea that Halloween night in October 1967 that it was to be the first day of the rest of my life. It certainly didn't seem like that to me.

I remember celebrating the anniversary of our meeting two years ago in New York. We were sitting at that fabulous table with the incredible view in the Rainbow Grill Bar with your sister Natalie, who was visiting with us. I recall looking out at the New York skyline. You ordered refills on the champagne and the hors d'oeuvres, and then you handed me a Movado watch that matched the one I'd given you for your birthday a couple of years earlier. And I laughed and said, "Well, there's no question that when we have it, we know how to spend it!"

And, it was true. As soon as the cash started flowing a little, out came the limos, luxury restaurants, hotels and shopping. We got such a kick out of it—buying nice things for each other. Only now I can't bring myself to give away all those clothes that so much remind me of the warm and vibrant you.

I just heard a commercial on television. It was about wife abuse—not physical, but emotional, psychological abuse. And the point it was making was that no man has the right to abuse a woman. Suddenly, it was Konny's voice, his berating, critical manner echoing in the words of the man in the commercial.

I never thought of it before, not even when, in Paris, Konny's daughter Cory had told me how frightened she had been of her father when she was a little girl because of all the tirades. But it makes sense—the way I felt, the lack of self-esteem, the anxiety, the feeling I could do nothing right, the inability to get out of the relationship, the manipulation, the apologies, the lavish gifts. I was in a psychologically abusive relationship and I didn't even know it—until this very day!

And the groundwork had been laid by my mother with her constant criticism, the perpetual belittling of all my dreams. She raised me in the contradictory atmosphere of considering me a genius and an idiot at the same time. She and Konny both made me feel responsible for all their ills and unhappiness, not to mention those of the world. And I was ripe to let them—the perfect victim. No wonder I was so insecure. No wonder I couldn't go for a job interview when you met me. No wonder I sneaked out of the first marriage just leaving a note. And no wonder I once even thought the only way out of a bad situation was to find another man. In Italy I was even ready to use my body to do that. (God, I remember those times and those foolish schemes. I was even stealing and stockpiling my mother's sleeping pills!) No wonder there was so much pain!

Not long ago I saw Zsa Zsa Gabor on a TV talk show. She was talking about the men in her life and repeating a conversation she'd had about one of them with some celebrity (Marlene Dietrich I think). The two women had discussed the fact that Zsa Zsa's man of the moment hit her. And the response from the other woman was, "He must love you a lot." The thing that struck me is I remember growing up myself with that mentality and those beliefs. How times have changed!

Beverly agrees with Gloria that your presence in the house is overwhelming. She meant the photos and the notes that are all over the place. "They're even in the laundry room," she said. I said, "Absolutely not!" I knew I had not put a picture of you in the laundry room! (Why would I do that? Who would ever see it? I haven't gone in there in years!) What it turned out to be was one of those stick-on labels that you get at conferences that says, "Hello: my name is" and you had written in "Norman." You had probably stuck it up there over the washing machine at some point. And, of course, I had left it there. But now I laugh when I visualize her opening the doors to do the laundry and almost hearing out loud, "Hello: my name is Norman!" She told me she really jumped the first time she saw it!

She also said that anybody taking me out—or trying to get interested—would be very intimidated sitting in our living room with the huge picture of you staring down at him from the mantelpiece.

I promised I would take it down before somebody came to pick me up. I know it's a little overbearing to have that photo of you on the mantelpiece (the enlargement we had made for the funeral). But until I go out on that date, I'd much rather look at your beautiful face than that rather bizarre, bleak landscape in the painting you bought at the Marina Art Show some 10 years ago which has dried out and is flaking away anyway.

You sometimes really surprised me and caught me off guard with your taste. Being the optimist that you are, you would read the most wonderful, positive messages into the strangest and most dour scenes!

Anyway, I know I should put your photos away and go on with my life. I'm just not sure what that means. You keep me company. You're my best friend. Why should I shut you away, close the door, when there's nothing here to take your place? I know some people will say that until I make the space available—no one can show up to fill it.

Meanwhile, I am beginning to tell friends that I'm available—at least to meet people, men, and we can take it from there. Joel and Michael did try to introduce me to somebody they had met, who has a background very similar to mine. They had a few friends over last Sunday—Estelle Getty, Rene and Albert Hague—and we all had a great time. But I think we really overwhelmed him with all our talk and inside jokes about the "business" and everything, and he turned out not to be right for me. But the fact that they thought to do that was very dear. (By the way, he's still wearing his wedding ring and it's been eight years! Actually, we're more alike than I realized.)

Unquestionably, it's chemistry that makes for physical attraction, breaks down barriers, and changes people. And love is irresistible. Being chased, pursued, wanted is a turn on. Being wanted by someone who turns you on too, is a powerful cause for "shifting gears." But I now understand Natalie's reluctance to go away for a weekend with that man she had met at the grief counseling group a couple of years ago. At the time I thought she was just being "old-fashioned." Now I can appreciate how very nerve-racking that choice can be.

≈ ~ ≈

Linda Lavin has a new show. It's called *Room for 2*.
Marty is the co-executive producer. It's about a widowed
mother and daughter who work together. Linda plays a
talk show hostess and her daughter is also her producer.
I happened to catch it last night quite by accident, and
the episode was about the second anniversary of the
husband's death. The daughter has made plans to "celebrate" her father's life with her mother (Linda) the way
they had done the previous year. But Linda has a date.
She explains to her daughter that she hadn't planned
to make the "celebration" a yearly event. Anyway, she
winds up kind of doing both. And when she's with the
guy, they have to play a game to try and get her not to
mention her husband in every sentence. (I know I do that,
too.)

Basically, she thinks she's all right. And then in the
theater it really gets to her. She starts to cry and she goes
back to her daughter's and explains that when her husband died she almost felt relief. She recounts all the
things she didn't have to put up with anymore. She says
that she thought she was ready to put it all behind her,
but now she has to admit that she misses him. And
then—later in the episode—on her show within a show,
Linda tells her audience a little anecdote about a flight
she took recently where she made friends with the
woman sitting next to her and they had a wonderful flight
together. When the plane landed they hugged, promised
to stay in touch, etc., and said a warm good-bye.

Then Linda went on to say, there was a delay in getting off the plane, and an interminable wait for the lug-
gage in the airport, and now she and the woman just

stood next to each other and looked out into space because there was nothing left to say. "You see," Linda concludes to her audience, "we made the mistake of saying good-bye too soon."

I'm not doing that, Normy. In fact, I don't know if I can say good-bye at all!

Letters to My Husband

My love—I miss you
  in the quiet of this afternoon
    with no sun in the sky
      I miss you.
Your phone call came
    bringing small comfort with it
      to know you are so far away.
Your voice—devoid of feeling
    because your heart is overflowing
      or because someone might be listening.
Tired, weary—my dear, sweet love
    because it's all too much.
I bring you comfort—yet sometimes pain.
    I lighten your burden, then read in your eyes
      I add to it.
If I stay the torment and torture will grow for us
    till they become too great to bear.
      If I go?—If I go?
Is the bond between us still loose enough to tear?
My love—I miss you
    Yet should I let you go?
      Now—before it's all too late.
Your life—so settled now
    could hurtle down a mountainside
      just like an avalanche
        because you love me.
      Should I let you go?
My love—I miss you
    softly now—yes, gently
      but soon
    the yearning may be too great to contain.
My love—I miss you.

Toronto, November 15, 1992

Normy,

I remember when I wrote that poem for you, my darling, more than two decades ago. We were going through so much heartache. You, because you were so torn between your needs and wants and your sense of obligation. Me, for some of the same reasons and because of your pain to boot.

It reminds me of one of the times we said good-bye. We were in Montauk, at Gurney's Inn (which is a spa now, I read somewhere). It was a cold wintry weekend, although it might even have been the month of May. I think it may have been Mother's Day.

It's funny how timing is everything in life. I was in my own apartment in New York by then, but you were still struggling with choices because when you were ready to get out, I hadn't been.

I had finally realized somewhere along the line that I needed to get myself straightened out and be my own person, or I would destroy our relationship like I had managed to do with all the rest. I recognized that I couldn't have left well enough alone; that somewhere along the line my "unworthiness" would have crept in and I would have started hurting and lashing out, and that would have been the beginning of the end for us.

So I had said to you, like Aldo had said to me some years before, "Don't do it for me. Do whatever you have to do for you."

· I explained to you that I had to get my head together—to see where that would take me. I had realized that I couldn't look for refuge in a relationship because I'd never find it there without finding myself first. I had understood that I had to come to a relationship, to you or whoever might be there for me, in strength, not in weakness. So, of course, your moment of daring had passed. (We run *to* something—not away—not even from pain.)

But we were still in love and had kept seeing each other, burning up the telephone wires, and racking up the airline miles, and every now and then agreeing that it was bringing too much pain.

So that weekend we talked and talked about the "right thing to do." Then you called home and after that we said good-bye and planned to go our separate ways.

Only like Mimi and Rodolfo in *La Boheme*, we decided to postpone the ending for just a little while. Until the morning when the sun could warm us as we said farewell.

God, how you held me tight that night! We never even made it into bed. After the talking and the phone calls, we lay down on the couch and listened to the sound of the ocean on the beach—each crashing wave emphasizing our distress and desperation. I was facing into the back of the couch and you hugged me from behind so tight I could barely breathe. And we lay like that, never moving. One massive ache till morning, when you drove me back to the city and went away.

I don't remember how long that separation lasted, but I suddenly realize how few of them were due to "ultimatums." Most of the time we were so keenly aware of each other's torment and needs. Most of the time, we were really friends, helping each other go through those very difficult times together.

It's funny how many of the poems, and the thoughts, and feelings I have now take me back to those early years with you.

I told Gloria that right after the funeral in L.A., I would be driving alone through the streets of Westwood and Beverly Hills, and I would get this eerie feeling that the last 15 years had never happened. That they didn't exist and that you were back home on San Ysidro and I was alone now because you had gone back to Anita.

And it's funny because in a way you have. I often wonder if she's up there with you. Ironically, apparently you have the same Hebrew *yahrzeit* date—although I'm not sure exactly how that could be—but Robin said she realized it when she got the notice from the mortuary.

It's funny the things that bring back memories and heighten pain. Music, for one, is lethal. It invokes the memories and underscores the longing. The songs that remind me of you and certain milestones in our relationship. Sometimes, here in Canada, I put on the news text channel and remember how you loved the background music they provided and how you used to leave the TV on while you worked on our books and correspondence in Calgary and Toronto. Hearing it makes me miss you so much. Like Roberta Flack says, the music is, "Killing me softly with his song...singing my life with his words..."

And beauty. The beauty of a clear blue sky, transparent water. A picture of a puppy, the wonders of the world...they still hurt, too.

Or Sundays. Rainy Sundays.

Bells ringing remind me of Rome. The past so vivid, my mind so "young." I don't feel like someone in middle age. I feel like I'm the same person who fell in love with you—just the other day, and yet it's years ago. Frequently when I'm in New York my mind seems to take me back to Konny, the apartment on Sutton Place, as if going back to that time will give me the opportunity to relive my relationship with you.

I was talking to Esther Silver at the beach last summer. The subject was aging and what a strange phenomena it is for all of us. She's a teacher and she says it's really hard for her to focus on the fact that her students' parents are younger than she is. She never thinks of it that way until she's confronted by it. Me neither. It's hard for me to realize that almost everyone I associate with is almost 20 years younger than I am. I know exactly how she feels. (And we also marveled at the fact that generally we have 10 times the energy that any of those "younger" folks do. How come? What's happening to people's drive these days?)

Simon MacCorkindale has a fan club and they send out a newsletter called *Simon Says*. There's a question-and-answer section, and one particular letter and Simon's response made me laugh, and underscored how silly and arbitrary I can sometimes be.

The question was, "This year, Fern Field is still listed as the Executive in Charge of Production, but her name now reads Fern Field Brooks. Did she get married during the hiatus?" Although we had never discussed this, Simon's reply was right on the money. He wrote, "Fern Field is indeed the Executive in Charge of Production, and the change in her credit is in memory of her husband Norman Brooks, who died in January 1991 before the second season began."

Boy, isn't that ironic? And isn't that just like me? Did she get married? No, she got widowed! That's why she changed, nay added, her husband's name! Honestly! Talk about too little, too late! You would have been so pleased and proud if I had done that while you were still living. But, no, ever since my divorce from Stan, I decided to keep my own name. Then, when you died, I felt compelled to use your name. Suddenly, I wanted the world to know that I was "Mrs. Norman Brooks." So, now that you're gone, my darling, half my credit cards and documents bear your name...and I never know who I am anymore.

But it's because I want to keep your memory alive, I want to feel you next to me. When you were here, I didn't have to do that because I had you. And I want you to know, my darling, that name or no name, I always loved you, more than I could ever say. Only, of course, you knew. That's one thing we always had—we knew how much we loved each other. (Even all those times we walked away.)

Another question in the newsletter was, "When CNN did that spot on the show while you were filming at Flushing Meadows during the U.S. Open, we saw a glimpse of an older, dark-haired lady who seemed to be directing the camera's movements. Was this Fern?" (Older, dark-haired lady? Are they talking about me?)

≈ ~ ≈

When I went to Carla's wedding, Carlo asked me, "Are you happy?" I looked at him. "Happy?" I responded. "No, I wouldn't say I'm happy. But I am okay, I'm okay." And I guess that's all I can ask to be.

≈ ~ ≈

Did I tell you about the *Bals des Casse-Pied*?

When I got back to Paris after the Christmas break last year, the whole city was covered with posters advertising this film called *Bals des Casse-Pied*. Literally translated, it means "The Ball of the Pains-in-the-Asses!"

How you would have laughed. Of course, we would have had to go to see it, even though it would have been entirely in French without English subtitles. I planned to go, but never got around to it. Still, every time I saw one of those posters, I shared a smile with you, and remembered how your personalized license plate, CASPIED, was born in a film theater on the Champs Élysées. You read a subtitle during *The Champ* as Jon Voight turned to Ricky Schroeder and told him he was a real pain-in-the-ass, and you fell in love with the word "casse-pied."

And I remember how you wouldn't tell me, and urged me to guess, what the "personalized" plates of our new Cadillac would be. (I also remember the irony of getting rid of my sportscar to buy a sensible four-door sedan so we wouldn't have to pry our mothers out of the back seat of your '69 Caddy convertible with a winch. Only they were both gone within nine months of our purchase.)

And how you teased me that I would never guess! And then one day, just before you got the plates, I was driving behind you and suddenly flashed on to the word "casse-pied," which we had started to call each other endearingly. I knew that that was what you had gotten as personalized plates and I won the bet! And we teased each other about whose car it really was and who was the real "casse-pied" in the family. "Piedo" it lovingly became. And how I wish you were here with me now, my darling "Piedo," my dearest "casse-pied."

I had CASPIED driven up here to Toronto figuring I don't need such a big car in L.A. anyway, and everyone says I'm ready for a new one, and maybe if I knew where I was going to be living, I would get serious about buying one. But I can't get any real money for it in L.A. Here I can lease it to the production companies I work for, make some money and then sell it. At least that was my rationale.

So the other day Keitha and her friend Andrew started talking to me about selling the car, and the tears welled up in my eyes, and my throat started to constrict. Sell our car? Sell CASPIED? How could I do that? It's a part of us! It represents our life together. Even if I take off our California plate and save it for another car when I go back to L.A., it will never be the same. It was one thing to talk about selling the car when it was in L.A. and

I was here. That was easy and seemed like a good idea, but now we're both in the same city, and it's just not so easy anymore.

And I've still got your convertible. I can't seem to bring myself to sell that either. It's running better than ever. I don't even mind taking it on the freeway. Well, maybe Mark will get his act together and one day I can give it to him, although I probably wouldn't be doing him any favors.

I asked Beverly to give your shoes to the homeless. Last year when I tried to do that, I couldn't. And the minute I heard she had done it, I wished I could get all of them back. I feel like I should have done it myself—said good-bye to each and every pair. Remembered how you loved this pair, how you had gotten those in Puerta Vallarta, how much you wore that pair. I should have gone through that ritual and not run away from it (another closure I just could not bear to face!). It will hurt when I get home and look at the empty holders, on the empty shelves in our half-empty closet. I will want to have them all back. I will want you back.

Normy, I remember seeing your toes that you hadn't shown me that December before you passed away. I remember the morning when I happened to glance at your feet and your toes were black and I flashed on to Jackie Gleason in that movie with Tom Hanks. He hid his feet from his son, because they were blackened from diabetes and I remember thinking, "But it hadn't been fatal." But then in the movies almost nothing ever is.

And when I asked you about it, you kind of shrugged it off (because you didn't want to worry me?). When you said it was circulation but that the color returned to normal as soon as you walked on the treadmill, I replied, "Then you should walk on the treadmill every day."

Charuzi was right. We didn't want to know. Would things be different today if we had gone to the doctor, confronted the gravity right there and then? Was I the one who wanted it to just go away?

I told Lois one of my other theories the last time I was in New York. That maybe you had chosen to die—to go now, because you were jealous. Because you were afraid I was going to have an affair. She doesn't think so. She thinks if that were the case, you would have stayed and fought. She asked me what I think you would have done if that had happened. I told her you always said if you ever found out I had been unfaithful, you would have killed me and the guy. She said, "Exactly. That's what I mean. Norman would never have thrown in the towel. He would have stayed to fight!"

I think that's true. I hope it's true. Come tell me that it is.

Toronto, November 22, 1992

Normele,

I was in New York last weekend. I took Elisabeth Getter to the theater for her birthday. We saw *Falsettos* and you can't help but think how the theater and times have changed in the last 20 years. Actually, how relationships have changed since then. Forget triangles where the husband leaves for the other woman. These days he's leaving for the other man!

(Thinking about how many things have changed just in our lifetime reminds me of an article I read recently in *Cosmopolitan* about a workshop being conducted on masturbation! And the writer observed, "If you can't do that in private—how in the world are you going to be able to do it in a group?" Good question! And how do you think our mothers would have reacted to something like that?!)

After the theater we went to the Algonquin, and God, that's changed too. Or at least, the ambiance and people seem different.

The other day on TV, there was a show about folks who have lived to be 100. There's getting to be more and more of them, and just think of all the changes they've witnessed in their lifetime! What do you think the next century will bring? How far off the mark do you think *Blade Runner* and *Star Wars* will be?

I also had a meeting about PR for this book. It's exciting and scary at the same time. You know how publicity always made me so uncomfortable. You always had to push and cajole me to talk to the press. Now I'll have to do that for myself, because promotion is part of being a successful writer. So I have to keep thinking positively and reminding myself this could be the beginning of a whole new career. A whole new life.

The PR company I met with asked me to send them some background information on me, our company, our projects. When I went through our press clippings it became so apparent how close we had been. (And also nice—some of the things people wrote about us—the worthwhile things that we did.)

All the stories talked about "us." One article starts out, "Producers Fern Field and Norman Brooks are best friends." Another is titled, "Producers With a Social Conscience." A third declares, "Field and Brooks Produce Togetherness."

Looking at all those stories and photographs, it became evident that the PR angle, the hook, now has to be "going it alone." Clearly, that's the path I have to travel. And, clearly, it's going to be a much bigger change than even I care to contemplate.

Oh, yes. I talked to Norman Lear the other day. He was so sweet. I was calling to tell him I'd seen his new show, *The Powers That Be*, and liked it, and that I'd caught some reruns of *All In The Family*, and how fabulous they all were. He was on his way out of his office, but said he got excited when he heard my name and wanted to say hello. I told him how I had recently been running into people we'd all worked with—and how every time that happened we all couldn't help but talk about "the good old days" and how wonderful they had been. We had truly been a family and he was the glue that held us all together.

He said he loved being back in production and perhaps he was building something over there at the studio and we could all be together again. Hal, Rod and Lorraine are working with him now.

Lorraine was vacationing in France last summer and came to visit. Hard to believe how her story has paralleled mine.

Remember, how shocked we were that cold December day reading about Pat Kenney's death in the old trades I had taken to New York with us. I remember you walking down the street and saying over and over again, "I feel so bad about Pat Kenney." And how sad we were when we finally got through to Lorraine on New Year's Day, and she told us about Pat's sudden heart attack. How he was dead by the time she got to the hospital from the office. He was just 64 (your age), had had two coronary operations (just like you), had died suddenly in November. Three days later, I called Lorraine and said, "Guess what happened to my Norman today."

≈ ~ ≈

I recently had dinner with Lynne Thomson. (Remember, we used her parents' house in *Kane & Abel* and gave her her first acting part?) I had her hysterically laughing about the time I decided we had to declare bankruptcy.

I had forgotten about it until I screened a documentary narrated by Jodie Foster called, *It Was a Wonderful Life*, about homeless women. But not the kind you see walking with shopping carts and looking like derelicts. The kind who live in their cars or shelters, but still have jobs and are clinging to a semblance of "respectability."

I've been wanting to do a movie on that subject for a long time now because a lot of people don't realize how easy it is to become homeless and fall off the edge.

Of course, hard for Lynne to understand because that will probably never be a problem for her, but I felt I knew first-hand how easily that could happen. I was explaining that when I first arrived in California it was easy for me to survive. I could do typing, teach languages, work several jobs. I could survive. It was when we started to make more money, got mortgages, had a bigger nut to crack, that things got sticky very quickly. When all you need is to cover rent, food and clothing it's not so bad. When you have to make $10,000 a month just to cover expenses (mortgages, salaries and office overhead), taking in typing, or doing translations, or even taking a night job isn't going to help.

And I started to tell her about those years right after the Writer's Guild strike, when we were hurting so badly. From expecting to have one of our best years to date, we wound up having one of our worst.

Earlier that year we had put our Palm Desert condo on the market, not because we needed the money then, but because we were no longer getting the use out of it that we should have. Six months later, we were hurting financially, had had no serious offers on it, and I, of course, was on the verge of a nervous breakdown.

You, in your infinite wisdom, simply raised the sale price of the condo! I went absolutely berserk.

I'm not sure even you really understood my psyche. By that summer, I was ready to stand on Monterey Avenue and simply beg anyone who would listen to me to please just take the condo off our hands. I would have given it away not to have that mortgage to worry about and the taxes hanging over our heads. Your philosophy, on the other hand, was always that things will work out. (And, of course, they usually did.)

Well, with a crazy optimist like that on my hands, I knew the only solution for us was to declare bankruptcy.

I'm sure I must have flung it in your face that I was going to get some info on it—and you probably handled it like you did all my *mishegas* (somehow the Yiddish word seems to convey far better than the English word "craziness" the extent of some of my "nutsiness"). You probably smiled and said, "Okay," because I don't remember any long discussions or any ranting and raving.

So I called a friend who was an attorney and asked her if she could recommend a bankruptcy lawyer for me. There was a long pause on the other end of the line (it was still the late '80s and people weren't declaring bankruptcy as frequently, or as easily, as they do now). Then she said she could give me the names of a couple of good bankruptcy attorneys, but would I mind answering a few questions first. I said, "Not at all." I'd tell her anything she wanted to know.

She started by asking if we had creditors dunning us. I said, "Not yet." She then asked if we had a lot of out-standing bills. I said, "No, just credit cards." (We were living off about 20 different accounts at the time and I had sold most of my gold jewelry to pay the mortgage that month, but I don't think I told her that.) She asked if they were in arrears. I had to admit they were current—we were paying the monthly minimums. "And don't you have some property?" she asked. I answered that we had the two condos, but probably not for long. She asked how many months behind in payment we were, and I had to confess that we were up-to-date.

She considered all this and then told me, almost apologetically, that she didn't think we were ready to declare bankruptcy, although I should feel free to pursue this with the attorneys she would recommend if I were so inclined. I didn't know whether to laugh or cry, and I don't remember if I felt peeved or pleased!

But I do remember hanging up the phone, almost dejectedly, and walking sheepishly into the den where you were sitting on the couch calmly reading the news-paper, probably trying hard not to laugh. When I looked at you I started to giggle, and you smiled, and I climbed onto the couch and into your arms, and we both had a good laugh, which was generally how all our major arguments wound up. And a month later you had made a great lease/option deal on the Palm Desert condo and I had landed a wonderful job.

But, it might have gone differently. It's not so hard to lose everything, to be left with nothing after years (it had happened to you, after all, though the circumstances had been very different). I remember finally asking you not long before you died why you didn't feel "poor" like I did.

I explained that the only thing I can relate to is income. It never mattered what else we had. I asked you how come the condos were assets to you when I saw them as "burdens," "liabilities." You explained that you felt you could always "liquidate." You might not get as much as you like, but you'd get something. I finally understood that on a gut level, but then the nagging thought came back—but what if they don't sell? Not for nothing did Konny once describe me as the "greengrocer's daughter," kidding me that I would never get rich because I wasn't willing to take the risks. And I guess that's very true—even though I have taken emotional risks that were far scarier. But I guess financial risk-taking has to be in the genes.

Not long ago on TV I heard a victim of Hurricane Andrew, which devastated Dade County in Florida this year. He was saying, "It's all gone," and then he corrected himself, "Not gone," he said, "we just have to start over. There's always tomorrow." God, the courage of ordinary people at times like that shines like a beacon.

Seriously though, while they did have a similarly bad storm early this century, it does feel like the predictions of the environmentalists are coming true—droughts, hurricanes, tornadoes, earthquakes. And still, saving the planet for our children seems to be a low priority! How can so many of us be so short-sighted as to think it's a choice between the environment or jobs? If we poison and destroy our environment there won't be any jobs to fill. Why is "making this world the very best place to live" so low on almost everyone's priority list?

And the politics—they've been a blast! It was a presidential election year and watching all those politicians this summer at the conventions just boggled the mind. But now we have a new president-elect—Governor Bill Clinton from Arkansas.

I got back from Europe just in time to catch the Republican convention on TV. The process was ludicrous. Nobody seemed to understand that our focus has to be people, not politics, pride not promises, talent not taxes.

And what company or organization do you know that would pay your salary and your expenses to let you go out and look for another job? When someone does that in the private sector, it's called unethical. When a public servant is running for another public office, it's standard operating procedure!

What company would let its president or CEO go on the road to visit other companies and campaign for another job? Not General Motors, not General Electric, certainly not Xerox or IBM. But our political system does just that. While President Bush and Governor Clinton are out campaigning, who's doing the jobs they're getting paid for? Does it make any sense at all?

I like my idea better. Politicians get to campaign the first time out. Then they run on their record and participate in some debates to defend it. After all, how many years do we need before we admit that campaign promises are just empty promises made to get the job.

I know a lot of my ideas about politics are farfetched and unconventional, but I see more and more of them being implemented and faring rather well.

Perot, in fact, seemed to be putting forth a lot of the ideas I have espoused for years. First of all, he paid for his own campaign. Second, he took it to the people. It was refreshing to see a businessman contrasting with the two politicians during the debates and the campaign. Trouble is none of them is even close to being ideal.

And maybe the government has become too big and too strong for anyone to bring it back into line. I remember the scariest line I learned in my Social Studies class at Columbia University was, "The system changes only enough to perpetuate itself."

Chilling, but it might be interesting to try to change it anyway.

It looks like Clinton has a shot at doing something like that. He and Al Gore looked good on the stage making their acceptance speeches on election night. It may be rejuvenating for the country to have a new generation in the White House. The world has undergone major changes in the last 50 years. Clinton and Gore and their children will be around long after most of today's politicians are gone. They have more at stake in the future of America and the world. Hopefully, they will protect it because it will be in their best interests and ours.

I guess we all think we can do a better job than the people we elect to represent us. That's why our series idea for "Ask The People" was a good one.

The trouble is that after we elect them, we forget they're working for us! And they forget it, too. They become members of some exclusive club on the Hill that removes them from the real world we live in.

As a child of refugee parents, my heart bleeds for America—the country my parents, especially my mother, loved more than life itself.

They had had to flee first Russia (because of the Communist Revolution), then Germany (because the Nazis were coming into their own), then France (because they never liked foreigners), then Italy (because Mussolini thought Hitler was going to win). America took them in and gave them a safe haven and they loved her for it.

When I said the Pledge of Allegiance as a little girl, it had special meaning for me. When my father wanted to move back to Europe after the war I was appalled. It wasn't even so much leaving my friends. It was leaving "my country." The only country, I thought, that stood for life, liberty and the pursuit of happiness. I used to defend it in heated arguments. When they told me France was a republic and had elections just like us, I thought they were lying to me! There could be no country that equalled my country, and certainly there was no city that rivaled my New York!

So maybe I was a little naive, and didn't have all the facts. But in those days, even as a little girl, I was a 110-percent New Yorker. When things got tough, New Yorkers got going. In the first blackout in the '60s, there was no crime in the city. New Yorkers reached out to each other and that was the way we were. Now New York is like a third-world country and there is no pride in anything. No pride in *your* street, no pride in *your* neighborhood, and therefore no pride in *your* city. We're losing the sense that this is *our* country, *our* city, and there are very few people trying the make this the best place it can be. What we've got are a lot of people struggling to survive, and the rest trying to see just how rich they can become.

Long before the Guardian Angels (which have fallen into some disfavor because of some publicity stunts and scams their leader has pulled), I was in favor of channeling the energies of gangs to doing good. The kids want to paint graffiti? Good. Let them paint rainbows instead. Surely there isn't a subway station in New York that couldn't use some attractive murals—and we'd discover some artistic talents clamoring for attention.

Let's shine the spotlight on the gangs and make them responsible for safety in their neighborhoods. Why were the Mafia strongholds of old the safest streets? Shine the spotlight on gangs who protect the old people in their neighborhoods, and name the safest street in the city after the most efficient leader of the best gang. I think we'll be surprised how far a little positive publicity will take us.

Make the budgets public, available for all to see. Make public servants accountable. That's what the title means—to serve the public.

When I was a little girl, Frank Sinatra made a short subject that won an Academy Award. It was called, "The House I Live In." The words went something like, "What is America to me? The house I live in, a plot of earth, a street, the butcher and the baker and the people that I meet—especially the people—that's America to me." They should reissue the film—and the song. People are hungry for something to believe in. Look at the people that flock to the televangelists. Look at their faces. Look at the cults, look at the gangs, then look at the faces of people in the newsreels paying homage to Hitler. The choice is in our hands. We can worship the golden calf and care only about the bottom line, and our own gratification—or we can rise to the occasion and make this the heaven on earth that it can be.

So, I've rambled on, my darling, but I do get carried away—swinging from my moods of extreme cynicism to the opposite when I know, if we had a good leader, our country would live up to its potential and we would all be proud to say, "I am an American."

St. Martin, November 30, 1992

My dear, sweet love,

This weekend I took Michael and Gloria to St. Martin for their birthdays. When I went to their party last August I wrote them a card that said:

> *"The good news is this card entitles you to*
> *an all-expense paid weekend for two anywhere*
> *in the world of your choosing.*
> *The bad news is—I'm coming with you!"*

So, first we thought Puerto Rico, but then Gloria's research indicated we should come here.

It's always good to see them, but poignant when Michael said to me—half-jokingly—that he's glad we don't do this more frequently and that he's glad he doesn't see me more often because it brings too much pain. When the three of us are together, he misses you too much. Especially on a trip like this.

I suppose it hit me that way, too, but I suppressed it until today. It seems I can always manage at first, but it only lasts for the first couple of days.

Gloria told me the funniest story the other day. When I was in New York not long ago, Sonny Grosso invited me to join him at his regular Monday night dinner party at Reo's. I don't know if you've ever been there (although, knowing you, you probably have). Anyway, it's a legendary restaurant, where everybody goes when they can get in. Sonny has his table there on Monday nights and the evenings are always great fun.

So that night I was there with Chris, a couple of other gentlemen from show business and Tony Lo Bianco with his gorgeous Italian girlfriend. She is very beautiful and the kind of woman you hate because she is so perfect you just know she wakes up in the morning looking just like that!

Anyway, I was seated next to Tony (I've been a fan of his for years) and we had the greatest time talking about the business, his writing and directing, and reminiscing about New York. He looked fabulous and the next day I told Gloria how much I had enjoyed myself, and how terrific I thought he was. Well, she got so excited, because this was the first time I had ever even mentioned another man in a positive light since you passed away. I told her to relax, he had this gorgeous girlfriend. "But they're not married," she said. "No, but they're an item, and she is stunning—and young. Who could compete?" Gloria was undaunted (with her looks, she can afford to be!) and wanted to know if I had given him my phone number. I told her I hadn't and mentioned that he hadn't asked, either. Well, she wasn't too happy about that.

So, the other day, she told me that a couple of weeks ago, while she was out on a modeling call, she was in this building downtown and went into the elevator, when who should walk in but Tony Lo Bianco. She was thrilled—not because she's a fan. Because she could talk to him about me!

So she turned to him and said, "I know you, you're Tony Lo Bianco. My friend, Fern Field, told me she had dinner with you and Sonny Grosso at Reo's and she had such a good time. She just thought you were terrific—smart and charming and..."

"Oh, yes," he said. "We did have a good time. Where is Fern?" "She's in Toronto," Gloria replied and would probably have given him my phone number right then and there, but I think one of them had reached their floor. Anyway, she said she was really pushing for me. She's not a Jewish mother for nothing!

$$\approx \sim \approx$$

Ready for this? The other night I dreamt of Ross Perot! I was working with him—in the television production business! You were in the dream, too, and Simon MacCorkindale and I don't know who else. It was a busy dream and Perot was acting impulsively, as usual. If I just mentioned NBC might be interested in a certain project, he was already on the phone, and I'm screaming, "Wait a minute—we have to talk! We're not ready." Then I woke up.

$$\approx \sim \approx$$

I don't care for St. Martin as much as I thought I would. It's not tropical enough, not varied enough, the snorkeling isn't good enough. But I think perhaps I'm looking for every tropical place to measure up to my dream memory of St. Croix in the '60s. I fell so in love with that island then that it will probably be hard for any place—even, or perhaps especially, the St. Croix of the '90s to measure up. But I do intend to visit there again because it has occurred to me that just like my heroine in *A Life of Her Own,* I could sever my ties, burn my bridges and go live on a tropical island—although everyone says I wouldn't last on one for very long. But how do they know—when I don't know?

When I'm in one of my more cynical frames of mind, when I think it's all hopeless, the thought of chucking it all in and becoming some kind of beach bum (albeit a geriatric one!) has a lot of appeal. Trouble is, these days you have to worry about safety, you have to worry about cost. Most of all, you have to make the decision to go, to get rid of everything and go—and for the moment, I seem to be unable to make those kinds of decisions altogether.

We also visited Anguilla one day where we had this great 82-year-old native cab driver, who took us on a tour of the island. With his toothless, wily grin, he told us the two greatest evils to ever beset humanity were "drugs and television." Needless to say, we agreed with him and I managed not to mention that I was a television producer currently working on an "action/adventure" series.

You read more and more about the health professionals' convictions that there is a connection between violence on television and in the movies and real life. I'm sure of it. And as our driver said, the combination of drugs, which has changed the nature of crime and society, and the increasing violence in our entertainment has ruined our world. Years ago, when we were lobbying for the integration of people with disabilities into the media, we were always quick to point out the power that it (the media) has. We would all cite the *Happy Days* library card incident, when the day after the Fonz took out a library card hundreds of thousands of young people did the same thing. We are quick to take the credit—yet just as quick to refute the blame.

And why are we surprised that our schools have turned into arsenals? Where were we as it was happening? It didn't happen overnight.

By the way, your lucky number—27—made me some money at roulette one night. And the funny thing was, when it came out, I knew it was coming out again. But of course, you know conservative me. Instead of letting all the money ride on it I took off the winnings and just let the original bet ride. Sure enough, 27 won again! Anyway, I made a small profit that night, thanks to you.

It's not the only time you've been there when I needed you. A couple of months ago, our lease-option tenant came back into the picture and the real estate agent called me with his offer on the Palm Desert condo. Well, when he had fallen out of escrow in the summer of '91, and moved out without even telling anybody, I took all the papers I had in Toronto back to L.A. figuring I didn't need them anymore.

So, although the offer did sound low to me, I had nothing to compare it to, and I said out loud that day in the office, "Normy, why aren't you here when I need you?"

That night, I was organizing your Running Mate, which Keitha suggested I use because it's smaller than my Day Runner and has that nice zipper all around it. And there, as I flipped a page, in your neat, precise, tiny handwriting was the whole lease-option purchase deal laid out for me: the opening offer, your counter, his, and the closing number with the agent's percentage—the works.

I was overwhelmed, then I smiled, looked up to heaven and said, "Thank you, Normy. I really needed these, and you were there for me—as always."

Norman, my love,

Tonight the world wears a shroud as the fog kisses my window panes and I can barely see the buildings and the lakeshore.

I've always loved the fog, except for the fog in San Francisco that pervaded the city at night when I was there with Konny sometime in the '60s. There was something ominous about that fog. Like John Carpenter's film *The Fog*. Or perhaps it was that everything in my life was negative then. But it was different from other fogs I've know in my time. Like the one in Rome, which is a soft, sensuous fog that rolls in just before the first morning light and caresses and envelopes you in its embrace. And then there's the L.A. fog, which is not so much full of personality as it is spectacular! I remember one night driving to visit a friend to commiserate with her about you (I think it was after Madrid and we weren't seeing each other). The fog was so thick I could not see the front end of my own car! And another night when I looked out from my 16th-floor window and the fog was so low to the ground that I couldn't see the street or buildings below me, but at my level, and above, it was clear and the sky was full of stars. A golden angel (that I knew was at the top of the Mormon Tabernacle Church Spire, which was completely hidden from sight by the dense fog) seemed to be floating in the air. It looked like he had just descended from the sky to walk on the cloudy carpet that covered the city.

St. Martin seems very far away from this winter wonderland—except for the mosquito bites that cover my back and legs. It seems ever since Positano, the mosquitoes have a field day (no pun intended) every time I land on one of their beautiful beachheads. I read recently that certain people attract them more than others. It seems certain blood types, or whatever, send out a scent of some kind. So, you see, even if I'm not sending out missives to the opposite sex, apparently the mosquitoes are getting the message loud and clear.

They never used to bother you very much, except that time when we were staying with Carlo and Titti at their home in Bagni di Tivoli. A mosquito got you and because of your anticoagulating medication a huge hematoma formed on your leg. It finally, mostly, went away, but there was some discoloration left on your leg to your dying day!

≈ ~ ≈

I've been refinancing both condos and the other day I got some kind of notice about an old loan on the Marina condo. It showed a lot of strange names and I immediately thought I had lost possession because someone had forgotten to pay a tax bill or something. I could remember reading those stories about people who lose their homes because some tax bill is overlooked and they never know they're in trouble until someone shows up with a piece of paper ready to take possession. Jim Boyd was hysterical laughing when I told him. He couldn't believe that I actually thought I had lost our home. He told me not to forget to put that in my book. He's convinced I'm nuts anyway.

I've been thinking I might move to Toronto. It's geographically well located because it's only an hour from New York, and only seven hours from Europe. L.A. is so far from the rest of the world—and so full of you. I don't know how I'll feel when I'm back there, alone, with only my memories of you.

Toronto, December 11, 1992

Normy, my darling,

I just lost my security blanket—they've pulled the rug out from under me. Not that we didn't expect it. We did. At best there was never more than a 50-50 chance that *Counterstrike* would be renewed for another year. I received the news that there wouldn't be a fourth season with no emotion, really, but suddenly I realized here it was. The day I've been dreading. When I would have to face not being under pressure, under deadlines. As painful and aggravating as some of those days have been, I have always known they were a blessing because they were my ballast—as you had been—and I didn't have to face an empty world without work, without pressure, without you. Not that I don't have things to do. I've already got projects I'm developing—and this book. But that's scary, too. I know I'm coming to the end of it. That soon I will have to face the moment when I finish the last page.

It's been interesting these past few weeks. I've procrastinated—sharpened pencils, pushed papers, watched TV. It has been hard for me to sit down and write. I've been avoiding it. It has also been harder for me to get myself together here than it was in Paris. There, once I made up my mind that I was going to exercise, I got up every morning and walked to the gym. Here, there's an exercise room in the building and I can't get my act together to go more than two or three times a week! It's all about coming to the end of something...or rather realizing that it's going to be time to start something new.

Beverly and I talked about it, the day of reckoning, the last time I was home in L.A. I've been on the road for three years. There's still a lot to do, so much that needs to be taken care of. I'm still filling the emptiness with it. But I know that when all the boxes have been put away, when all your clothes have found new homes, and my things are in order, when there is nothing left that needs to be taken care of, I will be knocked for a loop that will send me spinning into the darkness I have been afraid to face. The darkness of a life without you.

Ann Shanks told me a funny story back when they took me to dinner in Cannes the first spring you were not here. She lost her first husband when she was a very young woman with two babies. So, she really had her hands full—taking care of the children and making a living. Then she met Bob and they were married and time went by. Then, 20 or 25 years into their relationship, they were having a particularly difficult time and she went to this psychiatrist for counseling. Well, the woman told her it was clear that she had never properly mourned her first husband. You know how funny Ann can be. And what a brilliant storyteller—she had Bob and me in stitches! Anyway, Ann explained, she had just paid this woman $150 an hour, so she wasn't about to ignore what she had learned. She went home, took out a photograph of her first husband, grabbed some Kleenex and locked herself in the bathroom, where she sat down on the toilet and prepared to "mourn" her husband properly. Except that only a few seconds into the teary discourse she was having with the photo, apologizing for not having "properly mourned" him, she realized how silly she must look. So she blew her nose, put the picture away—and she and Bob probably had a good laugh, which took care of whatever was ailing them. She made me laugh so hard the tears were streaming down my cheeks.

I read a brief article in *Hemisphere* magazine the other day. It was a column on personal growth by someone named Michael Novak and was titled, "Let the Questions In." It talks about how life these days in America seems to be designed not to "let the questions in." "It's so busy," he says, "it can rush us into death before we've had a chance to stop and think." He goes on to say that in an earlier era Blaise Pascal wrote that, "Life is a search for continual diversion." He explains that it is for "distraction, for keeping the mind occupied with superficial things, for keeping out the voices...the voices that ask questions. What am I doing on this planet, with the hot sun resting on my face, the wind blowing through my hair? Where am I going? What am I trying to accomplish with my life? Why am I here?"

Mr. Novak goes on to tell the story of a friend who was lecturing in Wisconsin and went for a walk through the fields in the afternoon—and he let the questions in and realized he had to make a whole new start.

I know my time is coming to "let the questions in." I hope the answers won't take too long to follow.

Los Angeles, December 20, 1992

My beautiful, wonderful love,

I flew in late Friday night. As usual, there was a story crisis on the show, so I had to delay my departure. But I didn't want to miss the baby's birthday. Your grand-daughter celebrated her first birthday yesterday. She is gorgeous. She is walking up a storm and has the sun-niest disposition—just like you. She loves to smile and I held her in my arms and danced to an Elvis Christmas song, and she was mesmerized. You would have been totally hooked by her. And Adam, he's incredible. Tall and lean and growing into a real heartbreaker.

When I walked into the closet and your shoes were gone, I knew I was right when I wrote you that I should have gone through that ritual myself. And when I looked and saw no suits hanging on the rack, the emptiness resounded in my whole body and I longed to have you close to me again.

I had lunch with Natalie yesterday and then we went to the baby's birthday party together. Ruth Davidson and her daughters Jill and Sharon were there—also Alisa and Jody. They are all so beautiful. And Alisa has a baby too. A little boy. Your daughter Robin flew down from Oak-land for the weekend. Your baby, your oldest daughter, is getting grey, my love. Hard to believe. She's finally

beginning to look like a grown-up, instead of a mischie-
vous tomboy. And Bobbi is beginning to look like a
cross between Sophia Loren and Anna Magnani—a real
"earth mother."

Marcy and Edgar had their yearly holiday brunch
today. Seeing them, my aunt and Lilyan reminded me
that on a Sunday exactly 39 years ago—still a teenager—
I married Stan in my uncle's home only a few blocks
away, and set out on the road that would eventually lead
me to you.

I dreamt of you last night. You looked so warm and
alive—and suddenly I realized that you were here again
and I slapped my face just like Macauley Culkin in the
ads for *Home Alone,* and went, "Oh my God! Now you
can read the book I'm writing about you and you will
know how much I love you!" I think you'd really like it,
Normy. I think you would respond the way you did
when I surprised you with the medley of international
love songs that I sang to you at your 60th birthday bash.
You were so totally surprised and so moved that I had
come out of a 25-year retirement from singing that after
I was finished you got up, kissed me and held me so tight
that the photos show the pressure of your fingers on my
back. You were crying quietly and looked at me the
same way you looked at me the first time I said to you,
in response to some comment you had made, that I had
been waiting for you all my life.

Too soon, my love. You left me much too soon.

Next week I have an appointment to make changes to my will. I try to do it annually since things are always changing. I created a revocable living trust after you died so when I go, things can be as simple as possible for all concerned. And I also made out a living will.

Ironically, I found a note from you to me among your papers attached to an ad about living wills in which you wrote, "Fernie—I want to make out one of these. I don't want to be kept alive by artificial means. I want to go in dignity."

Well, that you did, my darling. That you did. And how fortunate we were that you went quickly, without suffering. How many people we know who have gone on for years, severely paralyzed, unable to talk, or confined to their beds, and how lucky we were that we didn't need a living will for you. Because, of course, like so many other things in our life, you, we, had never gotten around to making one. Just like we never got around to updating our wills—not once in 10 years—and how much pain and anguish that caused, my love.

I remember how hurt I was when your mother didn't leave you, or me, any little thing—a souvenir, a memento, something that said, "I love you and know you cared." Yes, I know that Natalie gave us part of her spoon collection, but that's not the same. And it wasn't just for us that I was upset. I was hurt for Ellen, too. She had been so good to your mom all through the years. But most of all, it was the cold way in which it was conveyed. In the impersonal and often negative phrases of legalese. I understand that she thought Lauren was the neediest and everything should go to her. But not to leave anything specific, sentimental, to each of her children as a way to say good-bye just didn't make sense. She loved you all very much and I don't think she was angry at anybody. And hurting people's feelings was never her way.

It's interesting that the two professions—medicine and law—which deal with most of our human suffering are generally populated with insensitive practitioners only interested in doing their job "to the letter of the law" in order to get paid—or not to get sued.

Unfortunately, I forgot all about that, and your will was no exception. In fact, because it was so old, it cut to the quick. You see, it didn't reflect that your relationship with Robin had much improved since the days when you had executed it. The days when you were so hurt and angry because she would come into town and not even call and you would only hear about her trips in retrospect. It didn't say how much you loved your children, how much each and every one of them meant to you— more than you could tell them because so often their ways and means of doing things were so different from your own. So they'll never know about your pain, and your feelings of helplessness and guilt, and all the things you were too proud to say.

We forget, or never realize, that our wills are the last manifestation of our lives, and ourselves, that we give to our loved ones. We leave this very important task in the hands of attorneys—never known for their compassion— to represent us, to speak for us, we use their words and their expressions to make our last wishes known to those most dear to us! What a great tragedy and mistake.

I remember the project you were working on with some of your associates, the "family videohistories," so that when a person dies there would be a videocassette of him or her talking to the family. "The Gift of a Lifetime." We should have produced one for you, and yours.

And if not a videotape—at least a letter. A letter for each person you dearly loved. I would have liked something like that from my mother. When she saw I couldn't talk to her about her death, I wish she had written me a letter. A letter I could have read, and reread, and cherished.

If there is one thing I learned from the experience of the reading of your will, it's that I would urge each and every parent, each and every spouse, and even each and every child to write a letter. A kind of "In Case I Go Before You, There Are Some Things I Want You To Know—Some Things I Need To Say" type letter.

So instead of a "reading of the will," each heir would get a letter.

And the legal profession should change the cut-and-dried language they prescribe and recommend for testaments. People should express themselves, and explain themselves. Those words when read so coldly can cut to the quick. If the people mentioned in a will are close enough to receive something when we're gone, surely they mean enough to us to merit a personal farewell.

When we were making the film about Jim Oleske he said even if only two people learned something about pediatric AIDS it would have been worth the effort. I feel if only one person reading this book sits down and writes a letter to their loved ones—my efforts will have been worthwhile.

Los Angeles, December 22, 1992

Darling Norman,

Last year, at the beginning of the holiday season, I sat down in my dimly lit Parisian apartment, looked out at the gilded dome of the Invalides and wrote you the first letter that was the beginning of, and the inspiration for, this book. An endeavor that has brought you closer to me than ever in many ways...and has helped me through the days and nights of the new year. With you close to me I never walked alone. Now who will walk with me in this coming new year?

Today I met with Drs. Charuzi and Kaplan, and Marty Shapiro, to establish the Norman G. Brooks/Save A Heart Foundation Fellowship for Cardiac Research at Cedars-Sinai Medical Center. They're very excited about the prospect, as I am. Especially since Charuzi is leaving on the 28th to meet with the "alumni" of the program in Israel next week. There are about a dozen of them already. And they're doing good work. One of the fellows even came up with a new procedure that has become a part of the cardiac care at the hospital. The best thing about this foundation is that there is a one-on-one relationship. It's not a big, impersonal organization. I mean, I'll be able to meet with, talk to, the man or woman who is the recipient of your fellowship. I like that.

We reviewed the letter I'm going to send out, probably in March, perhaps on your birthday, announcing your fellowship, and rallying people to help me support the work of the foundation and raise enough money (we need $60,000 a year to support a fellow in the program) to present your grant in 1994. They liked the letter. I think you'll like it too.

Last year I ran an ad in *Variety* and *The Hollywood Reporter* to let everyone know about the memorial service we were holding. It said we love you and we miss you and included that photo of you from our shoot in Arrowhead on "The Day My Kid Went Punk." (You look so sweet, and so great in it. Not like a man fighting for every breath—the precursor of your valve replacement surgery.)

This January, the ads will introduce the first two charitable activities I've started in your name. They say, "We love you...we miss you...but you continue to touch our lives." And then it announces, "Beginning in 1993—The Norman G. Brooks/Save A Heart Foundation Fellowship for Cardiac Research at Cedars-Sinai Medical Center, and the Norman G. Brooks/Fern Field Brooks/WIFF Film Finishing Grant for projects on the environment."

This year's artwork will be a rendering of your photo done by an incredibly talented woman, Priscilla Tweed, who's a member of Simon's fan club and has done extraordinary sketches of him, Christopher Plummer and the entire *Counterstrike* cast.

~ ~ ~

Shortly after you passed away someone gave me an excerpt from an article that had appeared in *Thanatos* magazine in the fall of 1988. I kept it in my Day Runner to reread when I came home at the holiday break in production. I shared it with Sonny whose mom died last year.

You and Your Grief During the Holiday Season
by Alan D. Wolfelt, Ph.D.

With good reason, holiday seasons are often among the most difficult of times for people who have experienced the death of someone loved. Holidays are intended to be times of joy, family togetherness, gift-giving, and thankfulness. Yet, if someone in your life has died, holidays can also naturally bring times of sadness, loss, and emptiness.

The special occasion creates a focus for the sense of loss that is totally unlike the daily routine of living. Traditional times you have shared underscore the significance of loss—"Dad always cut the turkey while Mom took his picture for the family album."

The full sense of loss of someone loved never occurs all at once. The onset of the holiday season often makes you realize how much your life has changed by the loss. A person that has been a vital part of your life is no longer present. You have every right to have feelings of loss, emptiness and sadness. Unfortunately, many people surrounding you may try to take these feelings away. Friends, family, and sometimes even professional caregivers erroneously believe that their job is to distract you from these feelings. To "forget about it," or, worse yet to "try to be happy" is to minimize the profound loss you have experienced.

Perhaps your major need is to acknowledge and work to survive the naturalness of "holiday grief." Many people I have had the privilege of working with, as well as my own experience, suggest that for some of us the anticipation of the holiday is sometimes worse than the day itself. This speaks of the need to plan ahead in anticipation of this vulnerable period of time.

While there are no simple guidelines to follow that will make it easy to cope with your grief during the holiday season, hopefully the following suggestions will help you make your personal experience with holiday grief more tolerable.

Talk about your grief. *Some people think that not talking about thoughts and feelings of grief will make the pain go away. However, in reality you will help yourself heal by finding people who will listen and help you feel understood. Be tolerant of your inability to function at optimum levels during the holiday season. Your feelings of loss will probably leave you feeling fatigued and your energy level will naturally slow you down. Respect what your body and mind are telling you as you work to lower your expectations of operating at high levels of efficiency.*

Eliminate unnecessary stresses. *You will already feel stressed so there is no point in over-extending or over-committing yourself. While you don't want to isolate yourself, part of keeping your levels of stress in check is to respect your need to have time for yourself. Some people may try to "keep you busy" in an effort to distract you from your grief. Perhaps, you too will be tempted to keep so busy that you don't think about the person who has died. Experience suggests that "keeping busy" only increases stress and serves to postpone the need to talk out thoughts and feelings related to your grief.*

Be with people you find supportive and comforting. *Work to identify those people around you that understand that holiday seasons heighten your feelings of loss and allow you to talk about your experience. You don't need to be around people that want you to be miserable, however, you also don't need to be around people that want you to maintain a "happy face."*

Include the person's name who has died in your conversations during the holiday season. *If other people sense you are able to talk about the person, it may help them recognize your need to remember the joy of having loved the person who was an important part of your life.*

Do what is right for you during the holidays. *Well-meaning friends and family may try to prescribe to you what you should do during the holiday season, or more specifically, on the holiday itself. These people may assume that they know what is best for you. Discuss your plans with a trusted friend who won't judge the decisions you make about how and with whom you will spend your time. Talking about these decisions out loud often helps clarify what it is you do want to do during the holidays. As you become aware of your needs, share them with your friends and family.*

Do plan ahead. *Decide what family traditions you want to maintain and what new ones you may want to start. Knowing how you will structure your time tends to help you anticipate schedules rather than just letting things happen. During this normally painful time of grief, getting caught off-guard may result in feelings of panic, fear and anxiety. As you make your plans, you may want to build in structure, yet leave room to change plans, if you decide it has become appropriate to do so.*

Embrace your treasure of memories. *Perhaps one of the best legacies that exists after the death of one loved, are memories. Holidays always stimulate us to think of times past. So, instead of ignoring the memories that come to you, share them with understanding family and friends. Memories are often tinged with both happiness and sadness. If your memories bring laughter, let yourself smile, and if your memories bring sadness, let yourself cry. Memories that were made in love can never be taken away from you.*

Renew your resources for living. *Spend time thinking about your life as it relates to meaning and purpose. The death of one loved often creates opportunities to take inventory of one's life as related to the past, present, future. The combination of a holiday and the loss in your life will naturally result in self-questioning related to the meaning and purpose of life.*

Express your faith. *You may discover a renewed sense of long-held beliefs or the evolution of a new set of beliefs during this time. Again, find people who understand your need to talk about whatever seems important for you to consider. If your faith is important to you, perhaps you will want to attend a special holiday service.*

Final thoughts. *As people who have been blessed with the capacity to give and receive love, we are forever changed by the experience of death in our lives. We, as humans, do not get over our grief, but work to reconcile ourselves to living with it. Holidays naturally bring a resurgence of intense feelings of loss and sadness. To acknowledge and move toward these feelings is healthier than attempting to repress or deny them.*

Remember—don't let anyone take your grief away from you during the holiday season. Try to love yourself and allow yourself to be embraced by surrounding yourself with caring, compassionate people!

(Reprinted with permission by Alan D. Wolfelt, Ph.D., *Thanatos* magazine, Fall 1988.)

I went to see Joel Kimmel today. His father passed away a couple of weeks ago. It's had a profound effect on him. He really misses his dad, who was a lot like you. A cheerful soul who always looked on the bright side and went out of his way to be kind to people. We visited and when I left he gave me a copy of the eulogy that he had written for his father. He said he kept it in the piano bench (remember he bought my mom's piano from her when she moved into the retirement hotel)—next to the eulogy I had written for my mother. And, ever the comedy writer, he said we should be known as "Eulogies R Us." After rereading my mom's, and what Joel wrote for his father, I think he's right.

Mine was called, "Eulogy to a Friend." His is titled, "Things My Father Taught Me, by Herman's son, Joel."

March 1982

Eulogy to a Friend

When I told my husband, Norman, that I didn't want any eulogies today—just a simple religious ceremony—he looked at me a little funny. So I thought about it and decided it would be appropriate for me to say a few things in honor and in memory of my mother.

It had to be me because my mother would not have tolerated someone else getting up and talking about her as if they knew her intimately, when they didn't. Few people did.

My mother did not believe in funerals and cemeteries. She always suffered somewhat from claustrophobia and the thought of being buried in the ground appalled her. She also did not believe in the formalities of paying respect to the dead. She believed in paying respect to the living. Until a few short weeks before her strokes, my mother carried a signed letter in her wallet stating that in case of accident, she wanted to donate her eyes and other vital organs to persons in need so that even in death, she could celebrate life.

My mother was a principled person and a crusader. I am, too, on occasion. And my experience of her illness—as brief as it was—and her dying has caused me to make a commitment to improve and to change things for the time when the rest of us must face those same circumstances.

My mother often complained that things were "too big" in this country, too impersonal, that she couldn't find a doctor who would simply listen to her. She said we were great at doing operations, but heaven help you if you needed anything else. She was right.

For two short weeks I watched her doctors and the hospital staff in action and I was appalled. From the demeaning practice of calling everyone by their first name, to the contradictory approaches of the internists and the specialists, to the routine of administering tests without thought of why they are being done, to turning bedridden patients like pieces of meat, to a total denial of alternative methods of treatment and prevention, and an absolutely terrifying ignorance of the benefits of treating disabled patients in a loving home environment—there was not one single indication that my mother was being treated as a human being who was sick and dying, which is, after all, a normal part of living. She was a series of charts, graphs, scans, symptoms and syndromes. And the medical establishment's approach to that input did not vary one iota based on who the patient was. It happened to be a frail human being nearing 80. They would have acted the same if it had been a 6-month-old infant, a 20-year-old young adult, or a 50-year-old person in the prime of life.

If there are those of you who are thinking that a memorial service is no place for controversy, then you didn't know my mother very well. My mother is standing here next to me saying, "Thank God! She finally heard me." But I heard her all along. And much of the time I agreed with her. It's just that she was so adamant and so vehement in her emotional responses to everything that it was hard to agree, or help her, most of the time.

That's the unfortunate truth. My mother was not an easygoing person. She was difficult, demanding, opinionated, emotional, strong and independent. Part of a vanishing breed of Russian refugees that spawned the likes of David Sarnoff and Helena Rubenstein. People who survived by their wits and because of who and what they were—and so were totally committed to being true to themselves.

As my husband says, there was no grey for my mother. It was either black or white. If she liked you, she loved you. If she didn't, watch out. Politeness was not part of her makeup. She labeled it hypocrisy and recoiled from it. With my mother you knew exactly where you stood and she would say philosophically, "People either love me or hate me. I can't change who or what I am."

But with it all, what she was, was a friend. Over and over in the last few days I've heard she was special, she was elegant, she was unique. But more pointedly than anything I've heard—she was a friend. "She did more for me than my family," someone said to me. "I feel that I have lost a great friend." "She was there for me when I needed someone and I will never forget that," someone else said—and it's true. What my mother could be was a wonderful friend. If my mother felt you needed her, she would wipe your slate clean, set aside all her prejudices and judgments and draw on all her experiences, worldliness and suffering to give you comfort, understanding and support.

Not many people knew that. But those who did reach out for her were comforted and enriched.

And I always knew it. I always knew that no matter how often or how much we fought and disagreed, my mother was there for me.

Whether it was making costumes for the school play after a busy day at her office and taking care of my father and me, to feeding 20 kids after a ball game in a small three-room hotel apartment when only six had been expected, to juggling and entertaining my teen-age dates when I had overbooked myself, to telling me as a young woman the Russian proverb she so thoroughly lived and believed: "Bud kem hochish, no bud v'polneh." Be whoever you want to be—but be it completely.

In 1961, on her birthday, I gave my mother a gold medal, which she wore every day. It says, "For understanding above and beyond the call of duty."

She understood and cared about me above and beyond the call of duty. Her caring was so strong that she waited to have her stroke until we got back from a trip to New York so we wouldn't be inconvenienced.

She cared so much not to be a bother to us that she systematically disposed of all her things and put her affairs in order so it would be as easy as possible for me, even though I refused to discuss her death with her as she wanted—and I'm sorry for that.

And she cared enough to linger a week to give us the opportunity to make sure everything was in order—and so that we could say good-bye to her. She gave me time to tell her how much I loved her—which I didn't often say. She gave me time to find and reread to her one of only a handful of souvenirs she kept after disposing of everything else. It was a letter I had written to her in 1959—one of the turbulent times in my life. And I know now that in turbulent times in her life, she reached for it. It is a most appropriate eulogy, and, after a preamble, it goes like this:

I love you. That's what I'm really writing about. I don't often say it anymore, but then, it's just because I don't often feel like saying those things. I don't often have feelings (I guess because I try to kill my emotions so I won't be upset by things) and you've got to feel love. This is kind of a "love letter" and it may be strange coming from daughter to mother, but today I feel, I'm alive, and so I'm happy, sad, young, old, sentimental and materialistic all at once and I felt like telling you all these things.

It's a kind of thanks, I guess. You know that I've always appreciated you and have thought you did a great job as a mother. You must know because, if I didn't feel that way, I never would have confided so many things to you. And I have confided in you because always, at the most difficult times and in the most trying circumstances, you have been unbelievably great.

Really, although I may disagree and sometimes disapprove of the way you act, when I have needed you, you were always ready to comfort and help me in any way you could without pushing me (which I would have resented) and don't think I'm not aware of this and don't appreciate it. I do, even if I don't say so. But even if I don't, you can tell because the next time I need help I always come to you. I wouldn't do that if I didn't trust, appreciate and love you. Don't cry and carry on now. And remember, I just wanted to tell you all this because I do love you, but tomorrow I may not feel like saying it. So, just remember, I think you're a wonderful, wonderful mother, and I love you. And the next time you need to know, just take out this letter and reread it. I love you very, very much."

And if my mother was going to have a tombstone, the epitaph would say, "She really was—a friend."

December 1992

Things My Father Taught Me
by Herman's son, Joel

I am a very lucky person. Herman Kimmel was my father. Only one other person in the world can say that, and he knows how fortunate he is as well. Unfortunately we are here on a very solemn occasion. But funerals don't necessarily have to be lacking in a sense of celebration.

That is one of the things my father taught me.

Because the life that my father led—and encouraged his sons to lead—is one to be celebrated. He appreciated everything that was valuable in life, and I am not referring to money. People would often say, "It doesn't take much to make Herman happy." A cup of coffee didn't have to be a very good cup of coffee for Herman to say, "What a good cup of coffee." A nurse, or nurse's aide, didn't have to be a beauty for Herman to say, "Isn't she the prettiest little thing?" She didn't even have to be little. A concert or recital didn't have to be of Philharmonic quality for Herman to say, "Don't they make beautiful music?"

That is one of the things my father taught me.

Music. The trumpet. The march from Aida with its intricate "triple tonguing." I would watch him, whenever those familiar strains would come on the radio. He would hold his imaginary trumpet, duplicating the fingering, smiling with joy, just as proud as if he was one of his often told of "marching bands." He must have been quite the young gentleman, back then. Before most, if not all of us, knew him. A musician by nature and by training, playing in speakeasies and bands with musicians who would go on to achieve fame and stardom. But Herman did not follow that road. He did something that was even more important to him. He honored his family and did what was expected of him. Being a musician was not considered respectable for a nice, Jewish boy, and there was, after all, a "family business" to think of. So Herman respected tradition.

And so my father taught me.

My memories of growing up are rather vague, although I remember vividly my father's mother, Nana, and his sister Aunt Blanche. I remember their humor, their warmth, and the parties in their house in Westbury. Herman and Cora remained inseparable all of her life, and my father never complained about the things he had every reason to. My mother could be difficult, my father worked hard in his wife's family business, we never had any money to play with. But he accepted it all with dignity, good grace and gentleness that remained his gift until the very end. He sent both of his boys through college by making loans and sacrifices. And most important to us, he and my mother encouraged us to pursue our dreams. Herman never questioned that giving up his music for the retail business was appropriate for him. He also never questioned his boys when we decided the retail business was not for us.

But a wonderful lesson has been passed on from his years at Smiles Stores:

"Treat people well and they'll treat you well. Give a customer what they want and when they want it. You'll only do that in the long run anyway, so why not smile and be nice in the first place?"

The things my father taught me.

"How ya doin', Herman?" These are the words I heard every day when I had the privilege of spending time with my father. Every waitress, every volunteer at the hospital where my mother spent time, where Herman went on to become head of the volunteers, where Herman himself was later to be cared for. "How ya doin', Herman?" from the bank tellers, the neighbors, the doctors and the receptionists, all treated equally, all responding to his credo: "Smile and be nice in the first place."

He was surrounded by love, and he knew it, right up until the end. When my mother, Cora, died, Herman, grieving though he was, always took pride in saying that when her time came, she was comfortable, without pain and clean. The same, I am grateful to say, can be said of Herman.

We are all blessed to have known such a good guy, such a nice man, such a gentleman. And I would like to thank a few generous souls who were there for him and for us during those difficult final months, weeks, and days: our beloved cousin Audrey Chalfin and her husband, Hal, who will always remain our surrogate sister and brother; Herman's brother-in-law Lou Smiles, and nephew Mark Singer; Blanche Pizer; and all the incredibly compassionate staff of the Villa Maria nursing home where he spent his last days have phoned us personally—something they seldom do—to express their sympathy and to tell us what a kind and gentle father we had. Always a pleasure to be with. "People don't die any differently than they lived," they told us. "He was such a nice man. He must have been a wonderful father." I added, "he was also a terrific dancer."

My companion in life, Michael, has always said, "Your father knows the real secret of life—enjoy yourself, take what life deals you, and don't complain." Michael is right.

I have been comforted through all this by the love and support of my family, my friends and this quote from the filmmaker, Preston Sturges: "There is no tragedy in dying. The only tragedy is in not having lived." Herman lived a good life.

And if Herman leaves any legacy, it is these things he taught me. Along with the words "please," "thank you," and "I love you." And he also leaves two sons, gay and proud, who will do our best to respect the memory of our wonderful father whom we love and miss very much, Herman Selner Kimmel. How ya doin', Herman?

You too, my darling Norman, died the way you lived—gently, like quicksilver slipping through my fingers.

And it seems you and Herman shared a philosophy of life. You learned yours from your grandfather. I remember how you used to tell me, "You can get a lot more with honey than with vinegar. My zaydie taught me that." And you followed that rule. So you were the nice one and I was the bitch.

So many of us never have the heart-to-heart talk with our parents that we would have liked to have. Because it's hard—when someone is dying—to broach something that both parties know is being broached because the end is at hand. I regret not having done that with my mother. She wanted to.

And I regret not having talked about it with you. It would have given me something to hold on to.

Los Angeles, December 27, 1992

Dear Norman,

It's been such a strange time for me since I've been back this time. There's a ton of work, so much to do, because I've been on the road for three years. The first one with you—and then two without you. And it was only four short weeks between the time you died in New York and I was back in Toronto supervising the series.

Well, I've started to get the place organized, and the few short hours I've had at home, I've focused on that. I have not even turned on the TV, and tonight I found the best FM station that plays pretty music without too much talk. They've already played "The Wind Beneath My Wings," which is exactly what you were and are to me. And now Streisand is singing "The Way We Were." Oh, my darling, the wonderful way we were.

A funny—actually strange—thing happened today. This lovely gentleman (he's 84) came to pick up more of your clothes for the homeless. He came last year and when he saw your photo he said he knew you from the Temple and the Israel Levin Senior Citizen Center. Anyway, when he walked into the living room today he stopped short and asked if I had changed your picture on the mantelpiece. I said no, I hadn't. Why? He explained he was sure it had been much bigger.

"This photo feels like it's much smaller than the one you had last year," he said. I couldn't believe my ears. "Do you feel that way, too?" I gasped. Because I had had the same impression ever since I had arrived.

No, this isn't the first time I've been back home. But it is the first time I've felt that way about the photo, and here was this stranger confirming the way I felt. Last year the photo used to dominate the room—and now it feels as if it has shrunk in size. It's as if you're beginning to fade into the background, not looming so large in my life. But, if that's happening, it's not my choice—it's yours. I want you here next to me—in my heart, on my mind, under my skin, and as part of my soul. And why would this total stranger be aware of a change?

I've been going through more stuff—some of it yours, some of it mine, some of it from "us to us"— notes and memos from me to you and you to me. And there are a lot of laughs among the tears, my darling.

The tears came when I ran across some kind of questionnaire that you had filled out for a seminar you took. It was a behavior/personality assessment form, and you were asked to choose the adjectives that most closely described what you were like and then rank the other choices on a sliding scale. The first group of choices were: "stubborn, persuasive, gentle, humble." You chose "gentle" and I smiled as the tears rolled down my cheeks. Then I looked at the other words you selected: "adventurous, obliging, convincing, assertive." And, in the second place you selected: "persuasive, competitive, life-of-the-party, good-natured, optimistic." "Stubborn, obedient, precise, determined and accurate" were in third position, and "humble, playful, moderate, cautious and lenient" brought up the rear. Your children would certainly agree that "lenient" was never at the top of the list of your characteristics. And, yes, I would agree with all of your choices—but most of all with "gentle." My beautiful, loving husband. You were sweet, kind and, more than anything else, gentle.

The other night someone picked up the book that Philip had given you when you were going through all the trouble with your in-laws and the business. The title is *There Are Some Men Too Gentle to Live Among Wolves.* An apt tribute from one brother to another.

And then I ran across a piece of paper I had given you that you had dated 3/22/86. And I shook my head at how many times I must have been the bane of your existence.

It's handwritten, and obviously conceived during our economic "hard times." Never one to minimize things, I titled it a "Life Plan." Steps One and Two were labeled "long-range goals." The first was to move to the desert at age 65 (I assume that meant when *you* reached 65, not me) on an income of $50,000 a year. The second step was to take five years to make a nest egg of $500,000. I marvel now as I think of what we have managed to accumulate since then.

You see, my darling, it's just a little over five years and that goal (except for this damned recession we're in) could have been very close at hand. We almost made it. And then I thought about the fact that you always believed we would. The eternal optimist.

And then I looked at the third item on that piece of paper labeled "short-range goals" and burst out laughing.

Good old pessimistic me was at work again. Under "a" I had written, "Money to survive six months—where does it come from?"

Then I listed projects and activities that could provide some income—and it's interesting to see how many of them went into production: "The American Ticket," *Guilty of Innocence, The Fortunate Pilgrim.* Yet there I was in March of 1986, hanging by my fingernails while you waltzed through life trying to figure out how to keep your wife from going off the deep end. The two condos, two cars, fully staffed and equipped office making me feel bankrupt—making you feel rich. It's all always relative, isn't it? How did Sondheim put it? "Send in the clowns...don't bother, they're here."

And, last but not least, I had listed my suggestions for reducing expenses: "Lay off the staff; no alimony payments; housekeeper only once a week." And this one I really like because it obviously was going to serve the dual purpose of saving money and getting us back in shape: "no dinners or unnecessary lunches!" (I assume I meant no eating out in restaurants—not that I was about to starve us to death!) God, I must have made you crazy! It's not easy to live with someone who always thinks she's at the end of her rope, expecting catastrophe around every corner. How did you ever put up with me?

I also came across a very nice note following Jerry Buck's AP article about us, which was picked up even in

Canada. It's from that nice young lawyer in Toronto—the one who helped us when we were making the deal on the animation for "Kiddie Kingdom." It ends with "Hopefully, there will be a number of opportunities for us to work together in the future."

I did call him when I was looking for some legal advice about moving to Canada and learned he had passed away. It's so sad. He was such a nice, young, man. I wonder if it was AIDS?

And in a small, plastic bag I found postcards of Scotland (Nessie, Culloden, and the Island of Skye) and the invitation to Jean-Paul's wedding and a postcard from St. Loup. It's hard to believe that was the summer of 1990, and that you had less than half a year to live!

My sweet, darling husband, how you enjoyed every trip, every experience, every place we went, and everything we did. And I almost enjoyed them more through you and your enthusiasm than because of my own pleasure and experiences.

(The music that's been playing all night on the radio is incredible, so soft and sentimental. It reminds me a lot of the record collection I had and used to play in New York—which my friend and neighbor, Fred Becker, once called, "Songs to Commit Suicide By"!)

Los Angeles, January 1, 1993

My love,

It's the beginning of a new year, and who knows what this year will bring? At least it started with a laugh. Somebody in our Toronto production office faxed this:

For All Those Born Before 1945

Consider the changes we have witnessed: We were born before television, before penicillin, before polio shots, frozen foods, Xerox, plastic, contact lenses, Frisbees and the Pill. We were born before radar, credit cards, split atoms, laser beams and ball-point pens. Before pantyhose, dishwashers, clothes dryers, electric blankets, air conditioners, drip-dry clothes, and before men walked on the moon. We got married first and then lived together. How quaint can you be?

In our time, closets were for clothes, not "coming out of." Bunnies were small rabbits and rabbits were not Volkswagens. Designer jeans were scheming girls named Jean, and having a meaningful relationship meant getting along well with our cousins. We thought fast food was what you ate during Lent, and Outer Space was the back of the Roxy Theatre.

We were born before house-husbands, gay rights, computer dating, dual careers and commuter marriages. We were born before day-care centers, group therapy and nursing homes.

We never heard of FM radio, tape decks, electric typewriters, artificial hearts, word processors, yogurt and guys wearing earrings.

For us, time-sharing meant togetherness, not condominiums. A "chip" meant a piece of wood, hardware meant hardware, and software wasn't even a word.

In 1940, "made in Japan" meant JUNK and the term "making out" referred to how you did on your exams. Pizzas, McDonalds and instant coffee were unheard of. We hit the scene when there were 5 and 10 cent stores where you actually bought things for 5 and 10 cents. The Corner Store sold ice-cream cones for a nickel or a dime. For one nickel, you could ride a street car (trolley), make a phone call, buy a Pepsi, or purchase enough stamps to mail one letter and two postcards. You could buy a new Chevy Coupe for $600. Gas was 11 cents a gallon.

In our day cigarette smoking was fashionable. Grass was mowed and Coke was a drink. Pot was something you cooked in. Rock music was a Grandma's lullaby, and AIDS were the teacher's helpers.

We were certainly not born before the difference between the sexes was discovered, but we were surely born before the sex change. We made do with what we had, and we were the last generation that was so dumb as to think you needed a husband to have a baby. No wonder we are so confused and there is such a generation gap today.

The author of that is unknown—but one of our directors said something that should surely be included with all that:

He said he was old enough to remember when "water was clean and sex was dirty." Now "water is dirty and sex is deadly!"

God—it's true—how many changes we've seen in just our lifetime. Forget everything that's gone on since the century began!

There's a picture I cut out of a magazine on one of my flights not long ago because when I came across it, it took my breath away. It's a gorgeous photo of the mountains in Banff towering over a couple who are kissing passionately in the middle of a snow-covered field.

Turns out it's a scene being shot for the soap opera *Another World.* But it looks so much like you and me on that day a few years ago when we went looking for our dream chalet in the Canadian Rockies...before your chest pains and the shortness of breath.

I updated my will today—and if it doesn't happen before (although I'm sure it will), at least the Norman G. Brooks/Save A Heart Foundation Fellowship in Cardiac Research will be granted when I die. As I told you, it takes $60,000 to sponsor a doctor for a year in the program at Cedars-Sinai Medical Center. So far, we're about halfway there, but if I strike it rich—or find another series to work on—we'll be able to grant it in 1994. If not it will have to wait a couple of years. But I'm determined to make it happen on an ongoing basis.

Don McDaniel, the estate-planning attorney, likes me because he said in all the years he's been practicing, he never had anybody who bequeathed their stuffed animals in their will.

Can I help it if I continue to accumulate those cuddly creatures even after giving a batch away every time I move? And I have some really nice ones now. The gigantic panda you carried into the Garden Restaurant at the Century Plaza Hotel on my birthday while I was in the middle of a network meeting. And Henry, the cuddly lavender stuffed rabbit who portrayed Oleske's mascot in *The Littlest Victims*. I like him the best because he has a little pot belly and is so huggable, I hold him close every morning when I'm home. And there's the large St. Bernard Rod Parker, Jr., gave me on my birthday so very long ago.

Why shouldn't Children's Hospital get them? And do you think anybody will think of doing that if I'm not here and I don't say so?

Maria Stanfield was in from Atlanta and came to see me. She told me she worked again with Tim Matheson and when she went to pick him up at the airport, they talked of you and me. He remembered running into us at Angeli Mare just before we left for New York—how we had promised to call and get together. When he read of your death, he sent me a thoughtful note. Maria said she and Tim remembered the reaching out to others and love that you emanated.

I talked to Alan Gansburg the other day. He said he always remembered how you called him "Tatela"—and that he never knew exactly what it meant, but he always felt loved and it made him feel good when you said it.

I run across all sorts of things as I sort through the papers that still line every corner of your desk. There's a note from Edgar Rosenberg (Joan Rivers's husband) thanking us for the one we sent him after his bypass surgery, giving him the benefit of your post-operative perspective.

And a moving review by Adele Scheele of our "wellness" film. You know, Normy, we have done some pretty nice things.

When Adele stayed with me in Paris she noted that half my king-sized bed served as a catch-all desk and filing cabinet. She laughed and said she did that, too. She said it was a thing called "nesting." Apparently, it's something a lot of people do. I explained that I rarely move once I fall asleep. And, as an inveterate New Yorker, I'm trained to make the most of all available space.

At home, I sleep on your side of the bed, in the concave area your heavier frame carved out of our mattress. Actually, I guess we both worked on achieving that depression because I always slept as close to you as glue. Anyway, curled up like that in an almost fetal position leaves a lot of room that's wasted—so it's only natural to appropriate it for additional work space, which there never seems to be enough of in the house these days.

And then there are the cards—all over the place. From me to you and vice versa. Like the one with the two chubby, bundled-up people, hugging each other, that I thought we'd had for years. But it's dated December '90—it doesn't seem possible that you wrote "you" and "me" under the little figures just days before you passed away.

Or the one by Rick Norman (another Blue Mountain Arts card) that you gave me on my birthday in 1983 that says, "You are a part of me...a part that I could never live without. And I hope and pray that I never have to. I love you." And you are a part of me that I can't live without—only I have to.

And the one with the two old folks in the sailboat of life by Steven Kellogg "Wishing good luck and good health to a happy retirement" (and you wrote in "semi"). I guess that must have been in response to my "Life Plan" suggestions. You also handwrote a "thank you" to me for waiting for you "all of my life."

That really got to you—that phrase. I remember the day I first said it to you and the look of pleased wonder that came over your face. You had said something or other—I can't quite remember what—and I spontaneously blurted out that I had been "waiting for someone like you all of my life," and you just beamed!

Normy, my darling, my beloved,

How I've resisted sitting down to finish this book. I've done everything not to write because I had determined when I started this that I would end on the second anniversary of your death—which to me would really mark the first year of mourning. You see, I couldn't mourn during the first year because that was too painful, too devastating, too frightening.

And I thought by the time I finished writing this that I would have come further. That I would end this book by saying it's time to go on with my life—so, good-bye, my love.

Instead, just like your picture that seems to be getting smaller, less prominent in the house, I feel as if you're the one who's leaving, you're the one who's saying good-bye.

I've been aware for quite a while that I wasn't prepared to finish the book. I've watched myself procrastinate and find a million and one things that simply had to be done before I could concentrate on the book.

And it was interesting watching myself at home, back in L.A. at Christmas time—running, doing. I would come into the house and start right in, not turning on the TV or the radio—just sharing the house with my chores and my memories and thoughts of you. Knowing that soon—sooner than I want—there won't be anything left to do. There won't be any more boxes to go through, or clothes to give away, or things to straighten out, and then

I will no longer be able to live as if you were still here. I won't be able to pretend that you'll come walking through the door and smile at me and take me in your arms and hold me close.

I flew back here on January 3—the second anniversary of your death. And in a magazine I got at the airport, there's a review of a book called *Shadow Play* and a sidebar article titled, "Talking With...Charles Baxter." It's subtitled, "Writing to Fill a Hole In Your Life." Apparently the book is about the untimely death of a father, and the mother's retreat into madness. The author explains that "any terrible loss opens a hole in your life that you spend much of your time afterwards trying to fill."

I've just been through a whole two years when I didn't have to do that. The "hole" was filled with work, with crisis, with professional triumphs and disappointments. But soon it won't be. Soon I'll be with myself, alone—and I'll have to face what is going to be the rest of my life.

Normy, it's been two years, and I know the time has come to say good-bye. I just don't know if I can.

Remembrance
by Emily Brontë

Cold in the earth, and the deep snow piled above thee!
Far, far removed, cold in the dreary grave!
Have I forgot, my Only Love, to love thee,
Severed at last by Time's all-wearing wave?

Now, when alone, do my thoughts no longer hover
Over the mountains on Angora's shore;
Resting their wings where heath and fern-leaves cover
That noble heart for ever, ever more?

Cold in the earth, and fifteen wild Decembers
From those brown hills have melted into spring
Faithful indeed is the spirit that remembers
After such years of change and suffering!

Sweet Love of youth, forgive if I forgot thee
While the World's tide is bearing me along:
Sterner desires and darker hopes beset me,
Hopes which obscure but cannot do thee wrong.

No other Sun has lightened up my heaven;
No other Star has ever shone for me;
All my life's bliss from thy dear life was given
All my life's bliss is in the grave with thee.

But when the days of golden dreams had perished
And even Despair was powerless to destroy,
Then did I learn how existence could be cherished,
Strengthened and fed without the aid of joy;

Then did I check the tears of useless passion,
Weaned my young soul from yearning after thine;
Sternly denied its burning wish to hasten
Down to that tomb already more than mine!

And even yet, I dare not let it languish,
Dare not indulge in Memory's rapturous pain;
Once drinking deep of that divinest anguish,
How could I seek the empty world again?

Epilogue

Los Angeles, July 8, 1993

A note to my readers...

At the end of February, 1993, I returned to my home in Marina del Rey. I unpacked boxes and sorted files. I rearranged clothes closets and cleaned out drawers. And I faced the stark reality that my husband was no more.

I saw myself sink into the mire of indecision that is one of the characteristics of full-blown depression.

I explained to our psychologist friend Tom Backer, as I asked him for a referral, that this is me in a nervous breakdown. This is as bad as I get. I shower and dress, and answer the phone, and show up where I'm expected. But home alone, it's as bad as it can be.

I gathered names of support groups and phone numbers of grief counselors and diligently put them into my "To Do" file, but not into the pile of things marked, "To Do Today."

And I watched myself sit hunched over my kitchen table, nose buried in a book, as I shoveled food into my mouth with my bare fingers, and the house became more and more cluttered with things I didn't bother to put away. And I wondered if my next book would be titled *Descent Into Madness*.

But then I guess I decided not to go. Instead I finished this book, and started to explore what my future might be.

On May 13, which would have been our 14th wedding anniversary, I took off my wedding ring.

On May 18, I planned to give away the balance of Norman's clothes—but I just couldn't. So, I only gave away part of his things—and that was okay. Fortunately, he has a very large wardrobe. If I play my cards right, I can probably string this process out forever.

Today I'm getting dressed to go out on my first real "date."

And Normy doesn't know any of these things yet— so I know there will be "More Letters."

Thank you for sharing these with me.

Terri Field Brooks

Appendix

Legend—or how to find what you're looking for. If a person is mentioned in the book with just a first name—i.e., Aldo—look it up under the first letter of the *first* name. If a person is mentioned with first and last name—look it up under the first letter of the *last* name. Anyway—it's under one or the other. There wasn't enough room to include everything and everybody, but I'll be happy to explain any omissions. Drop me a note in care of the Career Press and I promise to get back to you.

ALDO: the second major love of my life. The man who changed my life forever and I will always love him for it. We are friends to this day.

GLORIA & MICHAEL ALHANTI: our best friends who had dinner with us the night Norman died. I called them right after my call to the paramedics, and they came to the hospital and took me home. I met Gloria in 1969 when I was hired by the small company she worked for and we discovered our lives paralleled each other's. I met Michael the first night they offered to drive me home, and as I sat down in the backseat and saw an artificial leg on the floor I asked flippantly, "Do you always carry a spare leg around?" And Michael answered just as lightly, "Yes, as a matter of fact, I do." Oops!

DENNIS & BEVERLY ALMACY: the good-looking Yosemite park ranger in a wheelchair who appeared in our short subject *It's a New Day...* He and his then-wife (they are now divorced) were also featured in our documentary on wellness for the California Department of Mental Health titled, *Just the Way You Are*.

JOAN ANTONUCCI: Robin's friend, who readily donated her blood in case Norman needed a transfusion during or after his coronary valve replacement surgery.

PETER ARBALLO: the good-looking guy in the wheelchair who started the whole ball rolling for the Media Office by challenging me to "do something" about integrating people with disabilities into the media.

LOREEN ARBUS: who with her husband, Norm Fox, helped put the Governor's Committee for Employment of the Handicapped Media Access Awards on the industry map. Within minutes after she joined the organization, we had every mover and shaker in Hollywood on our Dinner Committee for the Third Annual Awards Banquet.

ARRIGO BENVENUTI: well-known Florentine composer of 12-tone music. I met him when I was 16 and my parents and I stayed in his aunt's house in Montecatini, outside of Florence, where I studied singing for a while. He was a creative, crazy, musical genius. We stayed in touch through the years by mail. I saw him after many years—just before he died in 1992.

BEATRICE ARTHUR: star of *Maude* and *Golden Girls;* an animal activist; a champion of human rights; and always there when you need her.

TOM BACKER: psychologist and friend, with whom Norman produced an award-winning documentary, "The Dream's Not Enough," about four women with disabilities working in nontraditional professions. Tom has also invited us to participate in many conferences and seminars, including Mrs. Rosalyn Carter's Mental Health Symposium, which gave us the opportunity to meet Mrs. Carter and President Jimmy Carter. Norman was always full of wonder and excitement every time we did something like that.

DAN BIRMAN: a dear friend and colleague who began working for us after conferring an award on us in Huntington Beach for *A Different Approach.* A photographer and now a producer/director of documentary films, Dan worked for us in distribution, as a still photographer and cameraman. I love Dan, not only because he's been a caring friend over the years, but because no matter how hard the task, he always came up with a workable solution. Like when I asked him for a location that included a McDonald's from which we could shoot through the window to a bus-stop, where we needed a bus with a wheelchair lift. He got it all—no problem.

BOB: my cousin Lilyan's husband. He and Lilyan are responsible for several turns my life has taken. One was when I returned to the United States to attend their wedding after having lived in Europe. That brought me and Konny together. The next time was when Bob invited Norman to join us that fateful Halloween night in New York in 1967 and we met for the first time.

BRIAN and CHERYL: Norman's niece (Natalie's daughter) and her husband. Parents of Daniel, Esther and Lewis.

BRANKA: my friend for many years. We met in Rome when she worked for the Embassy. She played a major role in my separation from Konny, but that's a story for another book.

NEIL BUCHBINDER: the doctor who performed all of Norman's angiograms, and who was the one who prevailed upon us not to try to dissolve the blockage that was revealed in Norman's last angiogram in October of 1990. A decision I still think was the right one given the circumstances and the situation.

JERRY BUCK: a (now retired) reporter for the Associated Press wire service who did a nice story on us.

LOU CARILLO: the swarthy actor in a wheelchair who was featured in the musical number in *A Different Approach.*

CARLO & TITTI (MARIOTTI): my dear friends from the time when we were all young, carefree and living the high life in the magic that was Rome in the late '50s and '60s.

YZHAR CHARUZI: the clinical cardiologist Dr. Kuhn brought on to Norman's case when he was having his valve replacement surgery in 1987. He brought us great peace of mind with his almost compulsive dedication and reliable, twice-daily visits during Norman's post-surgical stay in the hospital. Norman continued to see him for his coronary care.

CHRIS (CHRISTINA KRAUSS): executive with Grosso-Jacobson/ *Counterstrike.*

CYRIELLE CLAIRE: the beautiful French star of stage and screen who was featured in the first season of *Counterstrike.*

GRAHAM COLE: one of an army of friends my darling husband made over the years in business and during his travels, who still remembers him fondly and therefore cares about me, too.

CORY: Konny's daughter—my stepdaughter for a brief period of time, and now a friend.

DANNY and JOYCE DEARDORFF: the super-talented singer/ composer/musician we featured at our second annual Governor's Committee Awards ceremony and his extraordinary wife who starred in a segment of *Just the Way You Are*, which we also released as a nine-minute theatrical short subject titled *Danny's Song*. They are now divorced.

JOHN DAVIDSON: popular singing star of the '70s and '80s, whose TV series included *The John Davidson Show* and *That's Incredible!* He would sometimes charter his incredibly gorgeous yacht, the Principia, which was anchored in the yacht harbor at Marina del Rey. We had planned to charter it when we found out Norman needed bypass surgery.

JEAN-JACQUES DEBOUT: composer/lyricist/director of the captivating megamusical *The Mysterious Voyage of Marie-Rose* and many other children's and adult's musicals, credited with a catalogue of over 300 songs. He began his career at 15 when he composed and sold his first song. Later he toured with Marlene Dietrich, and composed the song, and all subsequent musicals, that catapulted his wife, Chantal Goya, to fame as the Pied Piper of Paris preschoolers. Jean-Jacques has been called the Steven Spielberg of the French musical theater by the French press.

BONNY DORE: a wonderful producer and a dear friend, who was probably shocked when she mentioned she was getting married to Sandy Astor in France and I said, "We'll be there." And we were. It was a dream of a wedding—just as beautiful as they both are.

LARRY EISENBERG: friend, fellow temple member who, with his wife Alice and other volunteers (Hal and Jeanene Sloane, Al and Evey Friedkin and Annette and Earl Erdman among them), support the Creative Arts Temple/Israel Levin Breakfast program. On alternate Sundays they serve breakfast to senior citizens at the Venice-based Israel Levin Center, a program Norman participated in, supported and loved.

LILYAN EISENSTEIN: my cousin who's played a pivotal part in my life on many occasions. It was my mother's offer of a round-trip ticket to her wedding to Bob in 1961 that ended my residency in Europe and brought me back to New York, where I renewed my acquaintance with Konny. Bob was there the night I met Norman. Ironically, Bob died the day Norman probably got his coronary occlusion.

VINCENT FOURNIER: French-Canadian writer. He worked with us in Paris on *Counterstrike*. First person to read part of the manuscript for this book. His reaction encouraged me to proceed.

ALAN GANSBURG: reporter/writer/producer/director and friend who first interviewed us for *The Hollywood Reporter* when we were launching the Media Access Office.

ELISABETH GETTER: friend for many years, since we met in ballet class in New York when I was a teenage newlywed.

ESTELLE GETTY: dear friend whose credits include the Broadway award-winning show *Torch Song Trilogy* and who became the surprise hit on the TV series *Golden Girls*.

CHANTAL GOYA: French superstar of children's musicals who captured our imagination when we saw her performing on television in *The Mysterious Voyage of Marie-Rose* on French TV on Christmas Day in 1986.

MARCY & EDGAR GROSS: my cousin and her husband. She's a successful television producer. He's a business manager and feature film producer, with an elite, star-studded client roster.

SONNY GROSSO: former Italian-American street cop turned writer/producer. Partner to Eddie Eagen, the cop played by Gene Hackman in *The French Connection.* Roy Scheider played Sonny. Sonny's other credits include *The Seven-Ups*, and the television series *Top Cops*, *Nightheat*, *Diamonds*, *Secret Service* and *Counterstrike.*

RENE (ORIN) & ALBERT HAGUE: dear friends and neighbors who we met through our friend Larry Keith, when they came to California. Albert had been cast as Professor Sherovsky in the television series *Fame,* after playing the same part in the movie. He also played the part of a professor in the Afterschool Special I wrote, produced and directed entitled "The Day My Kid Went Punk." Acting was a late career change for Albert, who made his mark as a composer of Broadway shows. He's the winner of nine Tony Awards for *The Grinch Who Stole Christmas*, *Redhead*, *Plain & Fancy* and *The Great Magician.* Rene is an actress, singer and writer. We met Ann and Bob Shanks through them.

ADAM HAIGHT: the Canadian producer of *Counterstrike.*

HAL (COOPER): director of numerous pilots and TV sitcoms including *Maude; Dear John; Love, Sidney* and *The Powers That Be.*

BONNIE HAMMER: USA Networks executive who selected me to be the supervising producer of *The Ray Bradbury Theater*— which then led to *Counterstrike* and changed the direction of my professional career. She has become a dear friend.

KATHY HUDSON: the lovely lady who tends to our courtyard plants in Palm Desert with such tender loving care.

JEAN-PAUL: son of Chantal Goya and Jean-Jacques Debout. We attended his wedding at one of his parents' fabled castles at St. Loup in the heart of France.

JEAN-PIERRE (AVICE): business associate and friend since he was production manager for our Paris shoot of *Eleanor, First Lady of the World.* We've all moved up since then and his credits now include portions of James Bond movies, the Pink Panther movies, and such miniseries as *The Sun Also Rises, War and Remembrance* and *Kane & Abel.*

JEFF'S MOTHER (ETHEL GALLAGHER): kindly came every day to visit my mother after her stroke in 1982 while we were in New York on business. Jeff, her daughter, is married to our rabbi, Jerry Cutler, who, together with Norman and a bunch of other hardworking, dedicated people, founded the Creative Arts Temple (formerly Temple Sholem Aleichem). It was the first spin-off temple from the Synagogue for the Performing Arts, which Jerry Cutler also founded—and it was the first "show-biz" Temple in L.A. Now there are four, I think.

JERRY (CHERCHIO): owner of Jerry's Restaurant, an American hangout in Rome from the '50s to the '70s. I met him when I was 21 on my first night in Rome with my first husband Stan, when Aldo, whom we had met on the boat, wined and dined us until dawn. I saw Jerry just before he died in 1992.

JERRY (CUTLER): our friend and rabbi, who recruited Norman to be the founding president of our temple when we spun off from the Synagogue for the Performing Arts in 1980. It was an honor Norman, who had once studied to be a rabbi, was thrilled to have.

JOANN (ROTH): dear friend, caterer extraordinaire (Someone's In The Kitchen) and temple president after Norman. Married to Israeli artist Yossi Oseary.

MONIA JOBLIN: vice president of programming at USA Networks, who has become a friend since I began to work for them in 1990. We were with her on January 2 eating incredible homemade hot fudge—and less than 36 hours later she was at the hotel paying a condolence call. (She's often wondered if it was the richness of the fudge!)

SARAH JOBLIN: Monia's wonderful daughter who visited me with her mom when I lived in Paris.

JULIAN/JULIE: my first real love. We met in high school when I was 14 and he was 16. Broke up when I was 18. How different life would've been if we had wound up getting married. I think we'd still be together today.

KONNY KALSER: writer/producer/director—talented, successful filmmaker whom I first "picked up" in the lobby of the Sahara Hotel (or it might have been the Desert Sands) when Stan sent me away so I wouldn't disturb his gambling. Konny's mother, Irmgard von Cube, famed screenwriter of *Johnny Belinda* and *Mayerling*, got me my first movie part in the Mario Lanza/Renato Rascel film, *The Seven Hills of Rome* (*Arrivederci, Roma* in Italian, based on Rascel's song by the same name). Konny was the first to encourage me to become a writer and the first to condemn me when I did. He gave me my first opportunity to work behind the camera in film. Turned out he was a depressive personality I didn't know how to handle. A lot of good times—far outweighed by the bad times. We could've/should've been friends, never life partners. He passed away last July.

DR. LEO KAPLAN: the extraordinary octogenarian who heads up the Save a Heart Foundation.

LARRY KEITH: New York actor and former New York president of SAG. Our close friend since I hired him to star in *The Baxters* back in the early '80s. Had dinner with us and the Alhantis the night Norman died.

LORRAINE KENNEY: the best booth production assistant anyone ever had. She can knit, smoke, talk, take notes and time a show that's in progress, simultaneously and without skipping a beat.

PAT KENNEY: Lorraine's husband and CBS cameraman. He passed away several weeks before Norman under very similar circumstances.

JOEL KIMMEL: dear friend since our days working together on *The Baxters* when he and his then writing partner, Ann Gibbs, constituted the entire writing staff of the series. Together they've written for most TV series of the '80s (*Love Boat, Facts of Life, Webster*) and more recently Joel has written the successful one-man show about Oscar Levant titled *At Wit's End*, while Ann has revitalized her acting career. They both met when they were appearing in *Charlie Brown* on Broadway. Michael Peterson is Joel's significant other.

ROBERT KUHN: Norman's family doctor for many years, who I'm sure prolonged Norman's life with his diagnosis and timely recommendations in both the bypass surgery in 1980 and the valve replacement surgery in 1987.

NORMAN LEAR: friend, mentor, employer. Just an incredible human being. Also known for the shows that changed the face of TV in the '70s: *All In the Family, Good Times, Maude, The Jeffersons, One Day at a Time*, and many more.

LETIZIA: the woman who finally got Aldo (my second real love who changed my life) to say "I do." God only knows how she did it—I wasn't able to. Nor was anyone else in all the years since he split from his first wife way back in the '50s.

MARTY & ROCHELLE LITKE: close friends from New York who moved to L.A. shortly after I did. Rochelle and I used to be roommates in Manhattan—and it was she who accidentally found me the job with Norman Lear's Tandem production company while at a party in 1975. It was there she happened to meet a young woman who was leaving her job as assistant to Rod Parker, the executive producer of *Maude*. Two interviews and a week later I had the job, and the rest is history. My Norman and I were married in their beautiful backyard on May 13, 1979.

TONY LO BIANCO: star of numerous films and television shows including *The Seven-Ups*, *Blood Ties*, *City of Hope* and *F.I.S.T.* I've been a fan of his for years and wanted him to star in the first screenplay I ever wrote.

LOIS (DE LA HABA): New York literary agent. Friend for many years.

SOPHIA LOREN: even more beautiful in person than in her films. She's a wonderful cook and hostess to boot—not to mention a caring, fabulous mother. Star of the miniseries it took me 10 years to sell: Mario Puzo's *The Fortunate Pilgrim*. Won an Academy Award for her role in *Two Women* in 1961.

SIMON MacCORKINDALE: star of the television series *Counterstrike*, *Falcon Crest* and *Manimal*, as well as the films *Death on the Nile*, *Jesus of Nazareth* and *Jaws 3*. Married to Susan George, best known in the United States for her role opposite Dustin Hoffman in *Straw Dogs*, Sam Peckinpah's powerful film.

RICHARD MARCUS: friend and comedy writer who loved Norman and looked up to him as a father figure.

TIM MATHESON: sweet, caring human being who starred for us as Dr. James Oleske in *The Littlest Victims*. Other credits include *Animal House* and *To Be or Not to Be*.

JIM McMANUS: president of Radio City Music Hall Productions, who fell in love, as we did, with our children's megamusical, *The Mysterious Voyage of Marie-Rose*. As a result of trying to get that project off the ground, we shared many a magical evening together. He and his wife, Eileen, became our good friends. We were to have dinner with them the night after Norman died.

JOHN McPHERSON: shot *Eleanor, First Lady of the World* for me—although not the brief European shoot, because our budget wouldn't allow us to take our camera crew on location. Many years later he was the director of photography on *The Littlest Victims*, a film we did for CBS on HDTV (high definition television). It was on that shoot that he, and we, met Angela Mancuso. She, in turn, introduced me to Bonnie Hammer at USA Network, and three years of wonderful employment and friendship ensued from that introduction. John and Angela got married on New Year's Eve 1990 and Norman was their best man. Sadly, they read of his demise while on their honeymoon.

BEA MESHEKOW: friend and neighbor of Norman's since he moved into his house in L.A. back in the '50s. Their houses were so close that when he would sneeze, she'd call up and say "gesundheit."

MICHELE & MARTA: he is Aldo's cousin and a friend from the days when I lived in Rome with my first husband Stan. We met again at Carlo's house (another cousin of Aldo's and friend from that era) in L.A. many years later, at first not recognizing each other. In '88 we were their guests at a fabulous lobster dinner his Canadian wife, Marta, prepared with lobsters she had brought all the way from North America. Michele tells a funny story about how Marta tried to deny she had any lobsters with her when confronted by Italian customs over the open case of squirming crustaceans.

MICHELINE: Marcy Gross' cousin, but we call ourselves cousins, too. We've been friends since Micheline stayed with us for a month in Rome when I was a newlywed and she was 18. We had a grand time. She's beautiful, witty and has an elegance only French women possess.

NINA & MICHAEL (DAVID): my second cousin and her husband. Nina's father and my mother were cousins and grew up together in Russia. Nina's a research librarian. Michael's a playwright.

RICK NORMAN: greeting card artist who did one of the many cards Norman gave me.

JIM OLESKE: the incredible pediatrician and humanitarian portrayed in our film *The Littlest Victims* who's still fighting the good fight in the heart of Newark to win the battle against pediatric AIDS.

ROD PARKER: executive producer of *Maude*; *The Nancy Walker Show*; *Hot L Baltimore*; *Love, Sidney*; *Dear John* and *All's Fair*— and the best boss anyone ever had.

DAVID PERRY: my mother's younger brother, a self-made millionaire several times over. He was my favorite uncle—not only because he was so good-looking, but because I always knew he really liked me and respected me. He was a brilliant businessman and had a soft spot and a great sense of humor behind his gruff exterior. I loved him.

SYLVIN PERRY: my cousin who was with us the night I met Norman, and whose prodding to Norman on a subsequent occasion to "call my cousin—her husband's out-of-town" probably contributed to all that followed. We were all shocked by his untimely death from a heart attack at the age of 52.

DOROTHEA PETRIE: award-winning producer of television films. A caring, kind, gentle human being.

DORIS PHILBRICK: the lovely lady who traveled over an hour and a half each way to be in *A Different Approach* and one of our Governor's Committee Awards shows. She was grateful to us because she never dreamed after a bullet shattered her spine and put her in a wheelchair that she would ever be "dancing" in a film and on a stage. Some time after Norman died, I heard that Doris had passed away also. The world is a sadder place without her sunny smile.

CHRISTOPHER PLUMMER: star of stage, screen and television, with whom I worked on *Counterstrike*.

ETHEL POIRIER: she handled the nontheatrical distribution of our films. One of Norman's many "phone pals"—people he established close friendships with, sometimes without ever getting to see them in person.

SANDY POLLOCK: friend and publicist. She was able to get me a blowup of Norman's photo for the funeral at the eleventh hour so I could have people remember him the way he was in life—not in death.

MARIO PUZO: celebrated writer of *The Godfather* and numerous other works, including *The Fortunate Pilgrim* which I succeeded in packaging as a miniseries for NBC 10 years after first reading the book as a class assignment at a UCLA class on the history of the family.

GABRIELLA RANUCCI: friend of Carlo and Titti Mariotti who extended her hospitality to us at her stunning seaside villa south of Rome when we were vacationing in Italy in the summer of 1988.

PETER RICHE: the 32" tall person who roared into the auditions for *A Different Approach* behind the wheel of his imposing black Corvette. Both he and his car wound up in the film and we became fast friends. He even attended our wedding, but as we began to travel on location for various productions we lost touch. Some time after Norman died, I read Peter's obituary in the *L.A. Times*. He was a very special human being.

WENDY RICHE: our executive producer at ABC when we were working on a Special Olympics project with Bobby Shriver. Now executive producer of *General Hospital*.

NINA ROSENTHAL: former network executive who was our English dialigue coach during the last season of *Counterstrike*.

ROB & MONA MASSARO: dear friends who helped make my 50th birthday memorable on their wonderful 100-foot-plus yacht.

RUTH DAVIDSON: widow of Hy. Norman's relatives by his first marriage. Even though he didn't see them often in later years, he loved Hy very much and was devastated by his death.

HAL ROGERS: a dear man who may have helped me loosen my grip on my mother so she could embrace the death she longed for.

EDGAR ROSENBERG: Joan Rivers's late husband with whom I worked when they were developing a pilot for T.A.T. and I was head of development for the company.

PAUL RUDNICK: my internist since I moved to L.A. in the '70s and developed thyroid problems.

ADELE SCHEELE: career strategist, writer and broadcast journalist. A friend I met through professional circles many years ago.

BOB & ANN SHANKS: show biz couple par excellence. He wrote *Cool Fire*, created *Good Morning, America* and *20/20* and has written and produced numerous television movies. She's an award-winning photographer, writer/producer/director and whirlwind dynamo. She produced *Lillian* starring Zoe Caldwell and her books include *Old Is What You Get*, and a book on recycling garbage for children done way before its time in the '70s. We visited them in Sydney, Australia, while we were on location in New Zealand—and they have been concerned and caring friends to me during my period of mourning.

MARTY SHAPIRO: well-known L.A. agent and dedicated chairman of the Save a Heart Foundation.

ESTHER SILVER: friend of the Alhantis who verbalized the same feelings I had been having about growing old—we're doing it, but we're not "feeling" it.

KELLY SMITH: a colleague from my days at Norman Lear's, who also worked her way up through the ranks to become head of business affairs for the company.

STAN: my first husband. We met at Grossinger's in August when I was 19 and he was 33. We got engaged in September and were married in December. Although he was 14 years my senior, he never looked it. Didn't act it either. He could've had the perfect wife in me, but he didn't know how to get that, or keep it—so I grew up, he stayed the same and I left.

MARIA STANFIELD: the Italian-American young woman who worked for Tim Matheson while he was in Atlanta shooting *The Littlest Victims* for us.

JERRY STILLER & ANNE MEARA: We were staunch fans of these celebrities long before we met them through the Litke's and became friends. Though we don't often talk, they are always there when it matters—when Norman was in the hospital and after he died. They are caring, talented, dear people.

SY: my high-school steady who really loved me. But my heart belonged to Julie—who didn't care. Sy was the first one to awaken my sexuality, but of course, it was the '50s so we didn't "go all the way." I probably should have married him—at least he would never have accused me of being frigid like Stan did.

EDITH TAYLOR: woman I met when she was working for Konny years ago. It was she who recommended Dr. Johnson, the psychologist who made me "captain of my ship."

JOAN THORNTON: a colleague who had an eclectic group of friends including psychics, clairvoyants, psychologists and psychiatrists, some of whom gave me great comfort at the time of my mother's illness and subsequent death.

PRISCILLA TWEED: talented artist and member of Simon MacCorkindale's fan club. She used to send us the most incredible black and white sketches of the cast and did a rendering of Normy I used in the ads commemorating the second anniversary of his death.

ARTHUR WEINGARTEN: old acquaintance and new friend, whose enthusiasm for the first half of this book, which I gave him to read in 1992, thrilled and encouraged me because he was a "real" writer—someone who was a published author and had also been making a good living as a film and television writer. I had validation from someone I respected and wanted to consider a "peer."

ANNETTE ANDRÉ WEINGARTEN: Arthur's beautiful and talented actress wife whom I met on that infamous trip to London when I got nailed by the Paris customs official.

JACK (& PAM) WISHARD: former head of the Procter & Gamble production arm in L.A. We worked on a number of projects including the film *One Special Victory* based on the book *B-Ball—The Team That Never Lost a Game,* which starred John Larroquette.

YARA: my father's youngest sister, considered to be a tramp by my mother, whose greatest concern was that I would grow up to be just like my aunt. Since both women were volatile, typical Russians, they were always in competition with each other. My aunt tried to buy my loyalty with the promise of being her "only heir." My mother told her I couldn't be bought, and years later—after my mother passed away—my aunt realized what my mother had told her was true. So she disinherited me in favor of some people who were more likely prospects.

HOPE YASUI: the lovely lady who provided us with administrative support from the Governor's Committee in Sacramento for the Media Access Awards dinners.

A DIFFERENT APPROACH: the live-action short subject I produced and directed, which was nominated for an Academy Award.

"THE AMERICAN TICKET": a pilot I developed in 1986 for KCET to combat illiteracy. It finally developed into a sitcom, *The American Sign Factory.*

BROOKFIELD PRODUCTIONS: the company I formed with Norman in 1980 when we decided we wanted to spend as much time together as possible and not fight conflicting vacation schedules.

COUNTERSTRIKE: a Canadian/French co-production of a one-hour action-adventure series starring Christopher Plummer and Simon MacCorkindale, which was produced on location in Toronto and Paris by four production companies (Grosso-Jacobson, Alliance, Atlantique and Gaumont) for three broadcasters (USA, United States; CTV, Canada; and TF1, France). I was hired for the last nine episodes of season one and stayed for seasons two and three. Norman died during our Christmas hiatus between the first and second year—and I started writing this book during season two while living in Paris, where I spent 10 very healing months.

"THE DAY MY KID WENT PUNK": an ABC Afterschool Special that I wrote, produced and directed, originally titled "My Son, The Punker," (it was almost a condition of sale in those days at ABC that they got to change your title). When it aired in '87, it was highest rated ABC Afterschool Special to date and is still being used successfully in and out of the classroom to convey its message: It's what's on the inside, not the outside, that counts.

ELEANOR, FIRST LADY OF THE WORLD: CBS Movie-of-the-Week, starring Jean Stapleton, directed by John Erman, with teleplay by Caryl Ledner and Cynthia Mandelberg, from a story by Rhoda Lerman, which aired in 1982. This was my first real network prime-time producing credit.

THE FORTUNATE PILGRIM: a four-hour miniseries I packaged for NBC based on Mario Puzo's book of the same name. Project took 10 years from the day I wrote to Mr. Puzo after reading his wonderful book to seeing the show on air. Telecast as a five-hour miniseries in 1987.

GOLDEN GIRLS: popular sitcom created by Susan Harris, starring Beatrice Arthur, Rue McClanahan, Betty White and Estelle Getty.

GUILTY OF INNOCENCE: two-hour movie I produced for CBS about Lenell Geter, the Texas engineer who was erroneously arrested and spent 18 months in jail until a segment on *60 Minutes* forced the authorities to reopen the case.

HEARTSOUNDS: the remarkable 1984 movie adaptation, written for television by Fay Kanin, of Martha Lear's moving book about her husband Hal's five-year struggle with heart disease and the medical profession, as he goes from being a respected physician to a dying patient. James Garner and Mary Tyler Moore both received Emmy nominations and unanimous critical acclaim for their portrayals. Norman Lear, who was Hal's cousin, was executive producer and Glenn Jordan directed the film. To date, it is my favorite project of all time, and the irony is how close it paralleled my Norman's experience in many ways.

KANE & ABEL: the first miniseries I ever produced. A seven-hour epic based on Jeffrey Archer's blockbuster bestseller of the same name. Starring Peter Strauss and Sam Neill, it was the highest-rated miniseries of the season when it aired. CBS called and told us we had "saved the network." Michael Grade and Jud Kinberg exec-produced. Buzz Kulik directed.

"KIDDIE KINGDOM": charming children's series concept by Joe Shuster, the original creator of Superman, which we tried to produce together for many years.

A LIFE OF HER OWN: a one-hour, prime-time soap I wrote years ago in lieu of acting out my dream to go and settle on St. Croix.

THE LITTLEST VICTIMS: CBS Movie-of-the-Week we produced about Dr. James Oleske, a New Jersey pediatrician who was among the first to discover AIDS in babies.

MANY LIVES, MANY MASTERS: a book given to me by New York literary agent Lois de la Haba, written by a writer she represents, which fortified my feeling that I was left and Norman was taken because I still had work to do on this planet. Another incident that encouraged me to write this book.

THE MYSTERIOUS VOYAGE OF MARIE-ROSE: Children's mega-musical created by renowned French composer/lyricist/director Jean-Jacques Debout and made popular by his wife, international star Chantal Goya.

MR. WIZARD'S WORLD: the young people's science show created by Don Herbert, Mr. Wizard himself, which has been fascinating youngsters since 1951. I produced and co-directed one season in the early '80s when it was revived by Nickelodeon, the channel that put children's programming on the fast track. We taped at CFAC in Calgary, which introduced Norman and me to the incredible beauty of the Canadian Rockies, the glories of a 10 p.m. sunset and the intoxicating quality of clean air.

RAY BRADBURY THEATER: the half-hour dramatic series based on the short stories of world-renowned science-fiction writer Ray Bradbury, produced by Atlantis with various international partners.

WHY? BECAUSE WE LIKE YOU!: a TV movie about the Mickey Mouse Club that I was hired by Disney to produce. It never saw the light of day for a variety of reasons—none of them unusual in our business.

Author bio

Fern Field Brooks is an accomplished writer and producer. She began her career in the mid-1970s on Norman Lear's television series, _Maude_. She served as director of development for Lear's Embassy Television, then left to start her own company, and has developed, packaged, written, produced, directed and sold a number of movies, miniseries, sitcoms, soap operas, documentaries, children's programs and public service programs.

She is the recipient of a number of prestigious industry awards, including two George Foster Peabody Awards, an Oscar nomination, Emmy nominations, an NAACP Image Award and a Humanitas Award. In 1982, she received the Distinguished Service Award from the President of the United States.

Fern Field Brooks, like her late husband, Norman Brooks, has been praised for her efforts to further the interests of handicapped individuals in the entertainment industry. In 1978, she produced and directed the film _A Different Approach_, encouraging employment of the handicapped. She received an Oscar nomination and won 20 prestigious national and international awards, including the IFPA Best Directing Award.

She is a member of the Academy of Motion Picture Arts & Sciences, Academy of Television Arts & Sciences, the Caucus for Producers, Writers & Directors, as well as the WGA, DGA and PGA.

Born in Italy of Russian parents, she grew up in New York. She moved to Rome as a young newlywed to continue her operatic studies. After returning to New York, she spent several years working for an industrial film company. After meeting Norman Brooks in the mid-1970s, she moved to Los Angeles. She and Brooks had been married for 11 years when he died in 1991. _Letters to My Husband_ is Fern Field Brooks's first book.